R 200 399 8412

W9-BWA-520

I'VE GOT SAND IN
ALL THE WRONG PLACES

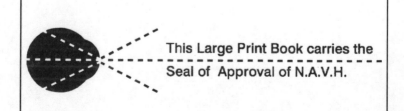

This Large Print Book carries the
Seal of Approval of N.A.V.H.

I'VE GOT SAND IN ALL THE WRONG PLACES

LISA SCOTTOLINE
& FRANCESCA SERRITELLA

THORNDIKE PRESS

A part of Gale, Cengage Learning

GALE
CENGAGE Learning®

Farmington Hills, Mich • San Francisco • New York • Waterville, Maine
Meriden, Conn • Mason, Ohio • Chicago

GALE
CENGAGE Learning·

LIBRARY OF CONGRESS CATALOGING-IN-PUBLICATION DATA

Names: Scottoline, Lisa, author. | Serritella, Francesca Scottoline, author.
Title: I've got sand in all the wrong places / by Lisa Scottoline & Francesca Serritella.
Description: Large print edition. | Waterville, Maine : Thorndike Press, 2016 | Thorndike press large print core
Identifiers: LCCN 2016020176 | ISBN 9781410491251 (hardcover) | ISBN 1410491250 (hardcover)
Subjects: LCSH: Mothers and daughters—Humor. | Women—Humor. | Scottoline, Lisa. | Serritella, Francesca Scottoline. | Large type books.
Classification: LCC PN6231.M68 S374 2016b | DDC 818/.602—dc23
LC record available at https://lccn.loc.gov/2016020176

Published in 2016 by arrangement with St. Martin's Press, LLC

Printed in the United States of America
1 2 3 4 5 6 7 20 19 18 17 16

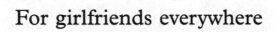

For girlfriends everywhere

CONTENTS

I'VE GOT SAND IN ALL THE WRONG PLACES

LISA

Who doesn't love summer?

It is our reward for three seasons of going full speed, twenty-four/seven, in a world that is too complex and way too fast.

We all need a break, especially mothers.

All year-round, we have to get everybody ready in the morning, while we pack lunches and find somebody's missing sneaker.

But it's summertime, and we get a breather and if we're lucky, an actual vacation.

During which we get everybody ready in the morning, while we pack lunches and find somebody's missing sneaker.

But at least we do it in a nicer place.

To me, the best part of summer is that the entire world relaxes just a bit, letting down mentally, easing off the gas emotionally.

That's what we all truly need, a July of the mind.

A time to wear mental flip-flops.

11

Fewer clothes.

More laughter.

An excess of wasted time.

Life, unplugged.

To me, the best part of summer is the beach.

It's all about the beach.

Every time I drive into a shore town, I can feel my mood lift and my spirit lighten.

I drive into town, past the saltwater-taffy and fudge stores, then the swirly-custard stands, fried-clam joints, and the drugstores that sell suntan lotion, where the only bottles left will have an SPF of 2 or 18326.

And nothing in between.

I know I'm at the beach when I pass my favorite store, which is the one that sells inflatable toys for kids, so outside will be oversized inflatable alligators, puffy rings like multicolored Life Savers, funky boogie boards, and foam noodles growing out of a barrel like so many Gerbera daisies.

Minus the Gerbera daisy part.

The salt air, the warm sun, the happy smiles; all of it is the stuff of summer.

And the great thing is, I feel that way whether I'm on vacation or not.

In fact, Francesca and I go on book tour every summer to promote these books, and even that feels like a vacation, just because it's summertime.

We drive around together, switching off on the driving and making our way through Rehoboth Beach, Bethany Beach, the Hamptons, Mystic, Connecticut, and Westerly, Rhode Island. We even took three ferries during our last tour, and this year we're expanding to Virginia Beach and Cape Cod beaches.

We might even take a paddleboat.

Why not?

It's summertime!

And that's the point of this little book, come to think of it. It's the seventh in this series, which Francesca and I have written about our lives alone and together, as mother and daughter. We're really ordinary and normal, and the more you read about us, the more you'll see your own life and your own families reflected herein.

Except that you probably behave better.

Because although our relationship is wonderful and we are truly each other's best friends, that doesn't mean we don't fight.

I'm here to say that we have fought our way through beaches along the East Coast and, as I mentioned above, we'll soon be expanding our fighting to Virginia and Massachusetts.

Yay!

Which brings me to my point.

Even in summertime, there will be problems.

You'll get in fights with your kids.

Or you'll get in fights with your mother or father.

Everybody knows that a family vacation is hardest on the family.

Also, things will go wrong, like the weather won't cooperate.

You'll find yourself with five days of vacation and four days of clouds, which means you'll stare at your phone, laptop, or television, mentally calculating how much it's costing you to be depressed in a new location.

Plus, you'll find yourself spending way too much time in the local grocery store, which will gouge you on price.

Also the drugstore, which will gouge you on price.

And any restaurant, which will gouge you on price.

Finally, you will get sand in all the wrong places.

You'll get sand in your sneakers.

You won't be able to shake all of it out.

You'll get sand stuck in the elastic in your bathing suit.

You won't be able to rinse all of it out.

You'll even get sand in your hair, blown by the wind off the sea onto your very scalp.

You won't be able to wash it out.

The sand will come back to the rental house with you, where it will fall on the floor, and when you drive home, it will be in the well underneath the gas pedal. You will track it inside your own house, and you will feel a grittiness under your toes in your very own bedroom, maybe even your sheets.

Don't let the sand bother you.

And above all, don't nag each other about it or whine about it, because that misses the point.

Flip it.

Think of the sand as fairy dust.

Because it is.

It's a magical sprinkling of a summertime mood.

If you're lucky, the sand will always be with you, wherever you go. A gritty little reminder under your feet.

And in your undies.

Summer is truly a state of mind.

If you keep that with you at all times — by that I mean, the mentally easing of worry, the emotional letting go, and more smiles in general — you will have a happier and healthier year.

Until summer rolls around again, and you

get to go back to the beach.
  To bring home more sand.
  Enjoy.

FIGHTING LIKE . . .
FRANCESCA

My kids are fighting.

They're not my kids, I should stop personifying them.

My cat is being mean to my son.

Sorry, my cat is being aggressive with my dog.

Like any parent knows, it's heartbreaking. It's keeping me up at night.

Literally. Last night at 2:45 A.M., a cat yowl woke me up. I had to take Pip into the bed for protective custody.

It wasn't always like this. A year and a half ago, I borrowed Mimi from my mother to catch a mouse in my apartment. But what was supposed to be a monthlong stay became permanent after I fell in love with this sweet, little, tuxedo cat.

Now she's just little and tuxedo.

Her bad cattitude came out of nowhere. My cat and dog used to get along perfectly. They cuddled together on my bed, he gave

17

her space, and she'd occasionally rub up against him.

Basically, they had my ideal relationship.

Until a month ago, when she started attacking him.

Can a cat have a midlife crisis?

Menopaws?

That pun deserves hissing.

Her mood swings come without warning. Pip will be minding his own business, padding toward the kitchen in hopes I'll feed him breakfast twice, when suddenly, Mimi will dart after him, chase him into a corner, and go full-blown cat-ninja on him, swiping

An uneasy truce

18

the air, caterwauling, and hissing.

Poor Pip never retaliates, he just scampers behind my legs like a frightened toddler, while Mimi saunters away.

She feels about as much guilt as Robert Durst.

I took Mimi to the vet, but she's perfectly healthy. The vet suggested she might be bored.

I didn't take offense.

But I've bought Mimi tons of toys since I got her, and the only game I've ever seen her enjoy is chasing after Pip's leash when it drags behind him.

I hoped this was more about the dragging

leash and less about tormenting Pip.

So I got crafty and made a custom lure out of ribbon for Mimi's cat teaser, a fishing pole–type toy. She seems entertained, but I think I'm more into it than she is. In an effort to tire her out, I find myself doing a full gymnastic ribbon-dancing routine.

I thought I was pretty good, too, but then my neighbors across the street held up two fives and a three.

Despite the increased playtime, Mimi still finds energy to lash out at the dog. So I decided instead of winding her up, I needed to help her unwind.

With recreational drugs.

I have dime bags of catnip stashed all over the house. Anything to keep it mellow when the cat's eyes look a little too focused.

We're not casual users anymore. I'm now growing "cosmic cat grass" on my windowsill, which is semi-legal in New York.

It's medicinal, okay?

But Mimi has the tolerance of Seth Rogen, because the vibes remain harsh.

Pip is normally calm and submissive, but now I see how anxious he's become, especially when the cat is nearby. Last week, I came home and found what looked like a scratch wound on his back.

The worst part is, this drama has manifested a secret fear I have about my ability to mother. I've always imagined myself having a child, specifically one child. I was an only child myself, but secretly, I have another reason:

I'm afraid I'll play favorites.

How can you not? But maybe it's the way I'm wired. I'm very loyal, I love fiercely, and my brain naturally categorizes things.

For instance, Mimi is my beloved cat.

But Pip is my baby.

My mom said she'd be happy to take Mimi back, but I can't give up on her. I do love her, and there was peace between them for so long, I have to think we can get back there.

And this morning, after another rough night, when I was browsing cat-behavior books online and feeling hopeless, Mimi leapt into my lap and began to purr.

She has a favorite, too.

LITTLE BLACK DRESS?
LISA

The Internet exploded over a dress, and my first thought was, who cares?

Until I figured out that I did, very much.

We begin when somebody on the Internet circulated a photo of a cocktail dress with horizontal stripes. The caption to the dress photo asked, What color is this dress?

I thought they were kidding, because the stripes were obviously black and blue.

So what?

I didn't really get it, and I certainly didn't share it because it wasn't very interesting. On the Internet, I only share really interesting things like adorable pictures of kittens and adorable pictures of puppies. On occasion I share adorable pictures of baby otters and baby squirrels, and occasionally a baby monkey.

If you're two months old and covered with fur, I'm your girl.

The only person I share anything with on

the Internet is Daughter Francesca, and she shares with me, too. Whether by nature or nurture, her tastes are similar, and so we often generate an electronic stream of adorable baby animals, crossing each other in email, undoubtedly colliding in the ether, but none of them hurting each other, because they're cute and cuddly and soft.

I didn't share the dress with her because I didn't care.

Then I noticed online, specifically on Facebook and Twitter, that not everybody saw the dress as black and blue. Some people thought it was white and gold. At first I thought they were kidding, so I went to look at the picture again, and oddly enough, the dress started looking white and gold to me.

Which was scary.

I didn't understand, and I like to understand, so then I started clicking on the articles about why we were all seeing the dress in different colors, and the articles explained something about rods and cones in the eye, and I got the gist, which was that everybody's eyes are different.

But then I started to notice online that people were taking sides. The people who saw the white-and-gold dress started finding each other online, and the people who saw the blue-and-black dress got together, and they formed teams, since they already had team colors.

And then, as the Internet would have it, they started yelling at each other, online. The white-and-gold people thought the blue-and-black people were wrong. The blue-and-black people thought the white-and-gold people were wrong. Then there was a third group who thought that this was too much yelling over a dress and it was really boring and it didn't make any sense.

I confess that I was in the last group.

I saw both colors, so I didn't like either team.

Plus I had better things to do in general.

Like my job.

I'm supposed to be in front of a computer writing a book, making my quota of two thousand words a day, and I'm happiest when I do that and don't find myself drawn into Internet feuds over clothes.

Then somebody online said that we should stop fighting about the dress because we all had more important things to worry about in the world.

I nodded yes.

Then I realized I was wrong.

The way everybody reacted to the dress is exactly what we should be worrying about in the world. In fact, it mirrors everything we're worried about in the world.

We tend to group around into teams, over shared beliefs. I think that's part of a human need to belong, and that can be a wonderful thing. Nothing feels better than sitting in a cheering section where everybody's wearing the same color jersey.

We are the champions, my friend!

But sometimes, we think that if the other team doesn't see things our way, the other team is wrong.

We forget that the difference in perspective is simply a difference, and not all differences are wrong.

Everybody's moral rods and cones are individual, and we will always see the world in different ways.

The important thing is to respect the views of others, even when we secretly think they have no idea what the hell they're talking about, or are completely and obviously wrong, or might even be out of their minds because the facts are so clear to anyone with half a brain.

It's a lot to learn from a dress.

Imagine what shoes have to teach us.

Ho Ho Ho
LISA

You might be reading this book in the summertime, but it chronicles a whole year in our lives, both the good and the bad, and beginning with the holidays, both the naughty and the nice.

What gets you in the mood?

I'm not talking about *that* mood, I'm talking about a holiday mood.

For the record, what gets me in *that* mood is Bradley Cooper, but I have a feeling I'm not getting him for Christmas.

Ho-ho-horny.

The holidays are upon us, and we're all performing the three hundred tasks required thereby, primarily shopping. So this year, to make my life easier, I had the great idea to do all my shopping online.

But, like many of my allegedly great ideas, it had a downside.

What happened was that my tour for my last book just ended, leaving me no time to go shopping, so I'd thought all online was the way to go. And I've just been online shopping for two hours, on the computer at my desk, where I sit every day, tapping on the keyboard, seeing no other human beings.

If you don't count a dog in a sweater.

Yes, my dogs wear sweaters this time of year, not only because I'm too cheap to turn up the heat, but also because they look completely adorable.

Plus I like dressing them in their sweaters because it makes me feel like I have children I don't have to send to college.

So to me, dogs in sweaters count as human beings.

Anyway, as regards online shopping, I got almost all of it done. I think I got pretty good deals, too, because it was so easy to switch around to the different websites and compare.

There was no rush for a parking space.

There were no long lines to wait in.

There was no begging a salesperson for a cardboard box.

There were no other shoppers, harried and exhausted, walking in circles around the mall, going through the same thing I was.

But now, two hours later, the disadvantage

is completely obvious.

I'm not in a holiday mood.

There is no holiday mood, anywhere in sight.

Why?

There was no rush for a parking space.

There were no long lines to wait in.

There was no begging a salesperson for a cardboard box.

There were no other shoppers, harried and exhausted, walking in circles around the mall, going through the same thing I was.

In short, I saved myself the time and the trouble, but the time and the trouble were exactly what put me in a holiday mood.

It turns out that a stress-free holiday is no holiday at all.

Maybe I have to hate the holiday to love the holiday?

It got me thinking about online shopping in general, and lately I've been thinking about that a lot, especially having been on book tour. It comes as no surprise to anyone that there are fewer bookstores in the world. Plenty of wonderful independent bookstores have closed, and even a big chain bookstore like Borders is now a thing of the past.

What worries me is that bookstores could become a thing of the past.

And if bookstores become a thing of the past, then it's only a matter of time until reading becomes a thing of the past.

And if that happens, I think we are worse for that, as a society.

It may be obvious as an abstract matter, but I realized that many other types of stores could go belly-up, if I keep shopping on my butt.

So I taught myself a lesson:

Vote with my feet.

If I want to live in a community that has bookstores and all other kinds of stores, as well as local people happily employed in those stores, I have to go out and buy stuff.

I'm putting on my coat and going shopping.

I look forward to the cranky shoppers, the waiting in lines, and the fighting over the parking space.

And I'm wishing you and yours a happily stressful holiday.

NOT A CREATURE
WAS STIRRING
LISA

Wanna hear what I got for Christmas?

Tularemia.

Don't know what that is?

Allow me to explain.

Rewind to a few days before Christmas, when Daughter Francesca came home for the holidays and was about to build us a fire, so I got in the car to go buy firewood since we didn't have any split logs.

I may be hardy but I don't know how to split logs.

I'm not a lumberjack, I just dress like one.

So I hop in the car and take off to the store, but I'm thirsty, plus I had a canker sore, which considering my pain threshold, feels like childbirth.

All week, I'd been painting my tongue with every canker-sore remedy they sell. I am the biggest baby on the planet, especially for mouth things, because they interfere with talking and eating, which are my hobbies.

To stay on point, I was in the car driving to the store, but I had left an open bottle of water in the cupholder from the day before, so I picked it up and took a gulp.

It tasted funny, but everything tastes funny, seasoned with Orajel.

Also it felt heavy, but I figured the water had frozen overnight.

Either way, I wasn't looking at the bottle, I was driving forward on my mission, with the task-oriented determination that women manifest at the holidays.

We get things done.

Stay out of our way.

Anyway, I drank the last of the water, tilting the bottle up, which was when I saw two black beady eyes staring back at me.

From inside the bottle.

The eyes belonged to a dead mouse.

In other words, there was a dead mouse inside the water bottle.

And I had drunk all the water.

Which the dead mouse had been marinating in, for a day.

Eeeewwwwwwwwwwww!

I started spitting, nearly avoiding driving off the road, and found myself at the traffic light, screaming inside my car.

People in other cars looked over, but

figured it was just another task-oriented woman at the holidays.

Then I did the only sensible thing, which was to call Francesca and wail, "I drank a mouse!"

And she said, "Eeeeeeeeewwwwwwww!"

Because I raised her right.

Don't ask me how a mouse got inside the bottle, or in my car. All I know is that I felt like barfing, but instead I hung up and kept driving to the store, where I bought the firewood and a bar of Hershey's chocolate with almonds, which I ate instantly.

Chocolate being the remedy for all things.

And also the cause of canker sores.

But never mind, I needed to feel good right away.

By the way, I also took a picture of the mouse in the bottle, because I knew no one would believe me, then I threw the bottled mouse away.

On the way home, I got a call back from Francesca. "Mom," she said, "you should call a doctor about the mouse."

"Why?"

"I was reading online that you can get bad things from drinking water contaminated with a dead mouse."

"Like, what? Nightmares?"

"No. Seriously, the mouse droppings in

Not the holiday surprise I was hoping for.

the water can cause disease."

"Really?"

I didn't believe her at first, but it turns out, the answer really is *really.*

I will spare you the details, but suffice it to say, 'twas the night before Christmas and all through the house, a creature was stirring, but it wasn't a mouse.

It was me, sitting on the toilet bowl.

All Christmas Eve.

Because of a mouse.

On Christmas morning, I called the doctor, who put me on a major antibiotic. He said that drinking water that contains a "mouse carcass" or droppings can cause an array of diseases, though they weren't generally seen in the Philadelphia suburbs.

Until now.

Go, me!

Well, as I write this, it's several days later. I'm beginning to feel better, and even my canker sore is gone.

Chocolate for everyone!

And Happy New Year!

Auld Lang Sayonara
FRANCESCA

The New Year is traditionally a sentimental, bittersweet, and reflective time. But upon reflection, all I can come up with is this:

Last year sucked.

Not for everyone. I sincerely hope that the past year was your best one yet, a harbinger of the even more amazing years you have in store. But if it was good to you, you're the exception that proves the rule. Unless you got engaged, married, or had a baby — in other words, everyone on my Facebook feed — it probably sucked.

International news was a parade of horrors. I don't want to get into it. There was nothing funny about it. If you don't believe me, think about it for one minute and then try not to hide under the covers.

Domestic news was a depressing series of lose-lose partisanship battles. Same as above.

Even Hollywood, Lalaland, a fantasy

world of money, glamour, and escapism could not escape the wrath of the last year.

Just ask Sony.

Or Bill Cosby, allegedly.

Or any starlet who thought the iCloud was private.

The year sucked for me personally. My beloved grandmother died, my boyfriend and I broke up, my dog had a limp, I gained weight, then lost weight — a nice end result but the process is not nearly as fun as gaining weight.

I could go on, but I'll spare you. I don't care to go over it myself. Suffice it to say:

It sucked.

I was a pickup short of a country song.

And I don't have a positive spin on it. There's no silver lining to not having my grandmother anymore. If you read us before, you know how much she meant to us. She was awesome and funny and cool, and I miss her all the time, but especially at the holidays. There's no silver lining to losing her.

Sometimes the only silver lining you get is to get through it.

So if you're at all like me, and you had a challenging year, I want to hug you and say this:

We made it.

And we all get a do-over starting next week.

Whether you envision the forward motion of the New Year as one foot in front of the other, or as my fantasy of being shot out of a cannon after lighting the fuse myself, let's embrace it.

Time marches on whether we like it or not. And this year, I like it.

My bad attitude is freeing. In my haste to put the past year behind me, I feel a good energy going into the New Year, or at least, an excess of it.

Pedal to the metal.

No looking back, eyes on the horizon.

I welcome the change, the unknown. Bring it on.

If I survived the last twelve months, then I'm bullet-proof.

This feeling was described to me back in 2008, when the author J. K. Rowling gave my college commencement address. In telling her story, she said:

"And so rock bottom became the solid foundation on which I rebuilt my life."

I love this idea. I've been working on a novel for years, but I've been too busy (read: too scared) to show it to anyone. What if they don't like it? What if it isn't good enough? What if I've wasted all this time?

That's last year talking.

Now I realize it can't get any less published than it is sitting on my computer.

An iCloud leak may actually improve my chances at achieving my dreams.

My impatience for the next step, for progress, for change, for *something,* now outweighs my fear of failure. I have nothing to lose.

That's the New Year talking.

I'm not saying it's easy to stir up optimism after a period when you're feeling down. But it's never easy. Even when things go perfectly, you can get scared. You get the feeling that one false move could mess it up, that you have to be careful.

But if your last year wasn't so great, be brave.

You don't like something about your life? Change it. Don't let another year go by before you try something different.

Because one year from now, on the next December 31, when we count down our good-bye to this year, you know what I want?

I want to miss it.

CHANGING TIDE
LISA

I get a lot of great fan mail, but sometimes it's less than adoring. For example, somebody recently wrote to me, "You call yourself 'middle-aged,' but you're already fifty-nine. Do you think you're going to live until you're 118?"

Not very nice.

But then again, absolutely true.

And though I generally don't pay attention to the occasional hater, this time I did. Maybe because her email arrived around the New Year, when we all think about the passage of time.

I considered her point, and it changed my mind.

I made a decision.

I won't call myself Middle-Aged anymore.

From now on, I'm going with New-and-Improved.

Because that's exactly how I feel.

Why should detergent have all the fun?

I'm at least as cool as a box of Tide.

Because age isn't about Age.

It's about how you feel inside.

I know I'm not the first person to have this thought, because we've all heard the expression, "You're as young as you feel."

But frankly, that expression never resonated with me.

Why?

The truth, at least for me, is that I don't feel Young.

And in my opinion, that's a good thing.

Let's get real.

I'm not going to lie to you.

(Because we weren't born yesterday. And how great is that?)

I know I'm not Young, physically. I own a mirror and I'm not delusional.

My body doesn't look the way it did when I was Young. I have more dimples, and not on my cheeks.

At least not *those* cheeks.

I also have a lot more laugh lines.

Because I've had a lot more laughs.

Years of them!

Which is great!

Plus, my body doesn't feel the way it used to when I was Young. My back aches in the morning, and I gain weight easier.

40

Not that gaining weight was ever a struggle.

We all have our cross to bear, and mine is chocolate cake.

My cross is a fork.

Yum.

The truth is I feel energetic, happy, and excited about life. These are characteristics of Young, but not all of Young.

At least not my Young.

When I was Young, I wasn't in control of my life. I didn't even try to be in control of my own life. I didn't make good decisions, I went along with letting others make decisions for me. I didn't have my own agenda, but I followed the agendas of others.

How do I know I did this?

When I was asked to do things, I could never say no.

I used to feel guilty when I said no.

I wanted to make everybody happy.

So I ended up fulfilling a million obligations that I didn't want to, and I turned my whole life into a Things To Do List.

And it wasn't even my Things To Do List. It was everybody else's.

It took me fifty years to figure out what I was doing wrong, and how to fix it. I started saying no, and the world did not end. Then I kept saying no, and it got easier and easier.

It takes practice.

All risk does, and all change. The more changes you make, the easier it is to change.

And I taught myself that every time I said no to someone else, I was saying yes to myself.

At the end of the day, some people still liked me, some didn't.

Either way, I didn't die.

On the contrary, I started living — my own life.

It was New for me, and definitely Improved.

So here we are.

If you used to call yourself Middle-Aged before, why don't you join me?

Let's change history.

Our own personal history.

We're all New-and-Improved!

LOVE MATCH
LISA

I don't want to ruin your undoubtedly excellent opinion of me, but there's something you should know.

I watch *The Bachelor.*

I confessed this to an author I know, and she said, "I get it, it's your guilty pleasure."

But she was wrong.

I don't feel guilty about it, at all.

In fact, I feel guilty if I miss it.

I told another author that I watch *The Bachelor,* and she said, "I understand, you hate-watch it."

But she was wrong, too.

I don't hate-watch anything.

If I hated something, I wouldn't watch it.

Just like food.

As in, I hate liver, so I don't eat it.

Who hate-eats liver?

Exactly.

Nobody.

So I don't hate-watch *The Bachelor,* and

on the contrary, I love-watch it.

I love, love, love-watch it.

Let's be real, I know a lot of women love *The Bachelor,* but I'm not sure many of them are in my age range.

New-and-Improved.

But so what?

You would think I'm supposed to be older and wiser, but age is giving me a perspective that there are no right answers, especially when it comes to love.

After all, I did everything right, or at least what right used to be before TV entered the dating picture. I met Thing One and Thing Two, spent a lot of time getting to know them, fell in love, got married, and then got divorced.

Who saw that coming?

Not me.

So who am I to say it's crazy to meet your husband on a TV show?

And even if you don't, it's fun for me to watch, and I love watching it.

Why?

People make out!

For starters.

In fact, as I'm writing this, the second episode just came on, and *The Bachelor,* an Iowa farmer named Chris, is about to go on a date with six women at once. And the women about to go on the date have just said, "I've never been this happy in my life," "I love Chris and he's amazing," and "I feel so lucky to have my first date with my future husband!"

Did I mention they have known him exactly one episode?

Excluding commercials.

But to be fair, it's a two-hour show, so you have to factor that in.

Like I said, I'm no expert, but maybe you should know someone for six episodes before you decide to marry him.

Then Chris sent them a note that said, "Show me your country," and the six women put on their bikinis.

Wait, that came out wrong.

And once the six women were properly dressed, they staged a tractor race in Los Angeles. The winner, Ashley, got to go on a date with Chris, which meant she sat on his lap and drank champagne while the other five women wished her dead.

Then Chris asked out Mackenzie, while the other women watched and said he was "such a gentleman."

That, I didn't agree with.

A real gentleman waits until you're out of the room to cheat on you.

The leftover women felt sad. One was

Tara, who got drunk, and said, "Tara always walks away empty-handed."

So now we know why she drinks.

To fill up her hands.

Though if you ask me, anyone who refers to themselves in the third person isn't drinking enough.

Chris took Mackenzie on a date and she told him she has a son and showed him a photo on her phone. Chris said her son is cute, and she said, "Chris has everything that I want in a guy and a father figure for my son."

You know what, that's as good a test as any.

Next, Chris flew on an airplane with Megan, but she didn't know where they were going. Megan didn't mind. She said, "I like a good mystery."

Yay!

I write good mysteries.

Think she reads me?

Or hate-reads me?

Later, they saw the Grand Canyon and had a picnic, after which Megan said, "Today, I am 100%, absolutely head over heels in love."

So am I.

With a TV show.

SWF Seeking Tamiflu

FRANCESCA

Last week, I had the flu.

Rather, the flu had me.

More accurately, the flu ran me over in a truck, reversed back over me, then sued me for bumper damage.

And I'm no baby when it comes to being sick. I've soldiered through many illnesses. I performed in my high-school musical with whooping cough, and I cracked two ribs from coughing. I had mono in college without knowing it.

I'm a tough cookie.

But the flu waged a sneak attack. It got me last Saturday when I was on a date.

As if a single girl in New York doesn't have it hard enough.

We were seeing a Russian film, and somewhere between the grim middle and the grimmer ending, my throat started to feel really sore. Then a splitting headache. Soon teeth-chattering chills.

I sent my date home without even a kiss on the cheek.

I'm great at playing hard to get with a temperature.

I thought it was a bad cold. I was sure my home-remedy voodoo would do the trick — neti pots and saltwater gargles, questionable uses for apple cider vinegar — but by Monday, I couldn't stand up without feeling faint.

And I live alone, with a cat.

(And a dog, but he's more likely to dial Domino's than 911.)

I'm at risk for Sad Single Lady Death. You know the fear. It's the reason we chew our food slowly and step carefully out of the shower. It's the nightmare scenario where you die alone in your apartment from something avoidable to non-spinsters, go undiscovered, and your cat does something that reveals it didn't really love you anyway, like eat your face.

I couldn't allow this cliché to come true. So I did something no twenty-something likes to do: I found a doctor.

All my friends are the same. We have every specialty doctor in the city — a gynecologist, a dermatologist; my one friend even has an acupuncturist — but none of us has a regular ol' general practitioner.

After much effort, I tracked down the number of a medical group, got an appointment, and dragged myself to the office.

Sitting in the waiting room, I had barely enough strength to fill out the paperwork. I slumped in the exam room, sunk into my puffy coat like a fallen soufflé.

I was expecting a Dr. Donna Edwards, but the doctor who walked in was a baby-faced young man.

"Dr. Edwards is the supervising physician," he explained. "I'm a resident."

I'm now at an age where it's possible that I am older than my doctor.

He evaluated me, which, judging by how God-awful I looked, didn't require a medical degree.

"Do you work in a school or busy office?" he asked.

"No, I work at home. I barely leave my apartment except to go to the gym."

"Probably caught a virus there."

The gym. I knew it. A health sham all along.

"Now this next thing," he began. "I could do it for you, but it'd be better for you if you do it yourself."

If only more men my age could admit that.

He handed me a long wooden Q-tip. "I need you to put this as far up your nose as

49

you're comfortable with, the farther the bet-ter."

He didn't know what a people-pleaser I was. I stuck that thing so far up, I touched my brain.

Five minutes later, I tested positive for Flu A.

I always was an A-student.

He prescribed Tamiflu. "It's an anti-retroviral."

I was horrified. "Like for AIDS?"

"Sorry, I mean anti-viral. I get those mixed up." He chuckled.

Adorable.

"Now it's not that common, but some people after taking this medication go into anaphylactic shock. So if you feel your throat closing, go to an ER."

Sad Single Lady Death!

"Well, I live alone, so how long do I have before I know if I have that reaction?"

"Not long."

I thanked him and left paler than before.

In the freezing rain, with only a fever to keep me warm, I had to walk from the doctor's office to the pharmacy, then to the grocery store. As I struggled to carry my heavy bags of canned soup, juice, and throat-healing sorbet, I thought:

This. Is. Really. Hard.

But I made it home. I took the Tamiflu and waited, eyeing my cat suspiciously.

I survived.

Hero Single Lady. Bona Fide New Yorker. Living Cat Owner.

I got through the flu. All by myself.

WITH APOLOGIES TO MOTHER MARY

LISA

I'm going to tell you about my most recent development in personal grooming.

I'll leave it to you to decide whether it's good or bad.

We begin with the basic facts, which are two:

It's cold out, and God invented fleece.

Let's be real.

As long as fleece exists, and it's cold out, it's hard to understand why anyone would wear anything else.

Or at least why I would.

In my own defense, I work at home, so I can get away with anything.

In other words, there's no dress code at my workplace, and no one around to fire me.

On the contrary, I'm always Employee of the Month.

The only other contenders are the dogs, and my novels are better than theirs.

Anyway, considering that I have no adult supervision, it was only natural that over time, I would dress down at work. It started with a fleece top and jeans, but pretty soon segued into a fleece top and fleece pants, plus fleece socks and a fleece hat.

Turns out that fleece is only a gateway drug.

Next thing you know, you're snorting lint.

I have gone from wearing only natural fibers to wearing only fake fibers. And one of my fleece tops is made from recycled water bottles.

Bottom line, I wear trash.

But in fairness, can you blame me?

What would you do if every day were Casual Friday?

A philosopher once said that the test of a man's character is what he does when no one is watching. But what about what he wears when no one is watching?

Or she?

Girls can be slobs, too.

That's what equal rights are all about.

Of course, it goes without saying that I'm braless.

As Daughter Francesca always says, Home Is Where the Bra Comes Off.

She's my favorite philosopher.

Still, she teases me when I'm wearing my

all-fleece ensemble, which she calls my teddy-bear clothes.

I'm fine with that.

I think I look huggable.

Oddly, no one is dating me, but I'm sure this is unrelated.

Which brings me to my current point, because in the old days, meaning last week, if I had to go to the store, or to the movies, or in public for any reason, I would change out of my teddy-bear clothes and put on jeans and a sweater, or something more presentable.

I figured that was what you were supposed to do.

It was like some line you should not cross, like a sound barrier of personal grooming.

I think I may have learned this from Mother Mary, who never liked my teddy-bear clothes. She always used to say, "You look like nobody cares."

To which I had no reply.

So you know where this is going.

Last Saturday night, I was getting ready to meet my best friend Franca at the movies, and I was about to change out of my teddy-bear clothes and into my normal clothes, when I stopped myself.

What was the point?

It was freezing outside, and my normal

clothes weren't as warm.

Also, we were going to the movies, where it was dark.

Plus, I usually keep my coat on at the movies, and my coat is knee length, so there was no chance anybody could see my clothes.

Finally, there are no single men left in the world, and even if there are, I wasn't going to run into them at the movies, because I never, ever have.

So I thought to myself:

GO FOR IT!

And I went to the movies in my teddy-bear clothes.

Braless.

I kept my coat on at first, but after a while, I took it off.

And you know what happened?

Nothing.

The world did not end.

Nobody threw up on sight.

I was happy and warm and comfy.

My breasts were happy and warm and comfy.

My jeans remained at home in the drawer.

And now, I decided that's where they're going to stay, all winter.

Hibernating.

Because nobody cares.

Except me.

But I care more about being happy and warm and comfy.

And in the end, that's a good thing.

THE STORM HAS PASSED
LISA

We know that last week's predicted monster winter storm did not happen.

What did happen, however, was a monster winter storm between Daughter Francesca and me.

We begin our story on a Friday night, when as usual, I'm home working on a book. This is not a complaint. I love my job, and wintertime is writing time for authors.

We hibernate like bears, only less smelly.

While I work, I keep the TV on in my office, and during the daytime, it's tuned to CNN because I'm a news junkie.

But by Friday afternoon, I was starting to hear the alarm creep into the commentators' voices, reporting about an upcoming snowstorm, which got my attention because it was about to hit New York, where Daughter Francesca lives. The TV was showing fast-moving white things, and the banners at the bottom of the screen were genuinely

alarming if you have given birth to somebody in New York City.

What's a mother to do?

Especially for a child who's not a child
anymore?

Remain Calm and Be Cool Mom.

So I played the part of Cool Mom but it
doesn't suit me.

By nightfall, I was Worried Mom, so I
texted her thusly:

"Hello darling daughter, this is Captain
Obvious texting you to tell you to get a lot
of food in the house because you're going
to get a big snowstorm. I love you very
much!"

Francesca texted back, "Okay, love you,
too!"

So far, so good.

But then during the late night, I began to
pay more attention to the banners on the
TV screen. They started as DANGEROUS
STORM TO BRING WHITE-OUT CON-
DITIONS, but I was not worrying, as
Francesca does not ski.

Then they morphed to NEW YORK
BRACES FOR EPIC SNOWSTORM, and
I worried a little more because "epic" is a
scary word.

When NY GOVERNOR DECLARES
STATE OF EMERGENCY popped onto

the screen, I got really worried because "state-of-emergency" is a scary phrase.

The only phrase scarier than state-of-emergency is "bikini-season."

I was getting more and more worried by the time we got to WORST OF MONSTER BLIZZARD ABOUT TO HIT NYC, and I completely panicked at COASTAL FLOODS AND HURRICANE FORCE WINDS PREDICTED. Francesca's apartment is near the river, and I was worried there was going to be another Hurricane Sandy.

So I became Hurricane Mom.

First thing in the morning, I called her, vaguely hysterical: "Honey, did you see the TV? There's going to be a big storm!"

"Don't worry, Mom," Francesca answered, too calmly for my taste.

"What are you doing? Did you go food shopping?"

"I'm working. I don't need to go food shopping. I have food in the fridge."

"But do you have canned goods?"

"Canned goods?" Francesca chuckled softly. "What are you talking about?"

"Canned goods, canned goods!"

Francesca replied, "I think I have a can of beans —"

"You need more beans, right away!"

"Why, what are you talking about? Please, you need to calm down."

"I can't! You need canned goods in case of a power outage! It's going to be a giant, epic, historic, emergency, monster blizzard storm!"

"They always say that."

"But they're right! This is CNN talking! Wolf Blitzer!"

"I'm okay."

"No, you're not! You're gonna DIE!"

So you know where this is going.

Drama ensued.

Voices were raised.

Things were said.

Tears were shed.

Mistakes were made.

Bottom line, there was a lot of passive voice happening, which is never a good thing, whether it's a federal government or a mother-daughter relationship.

But it had a happy ending.

There was no epic winter monster blizzard storm.

I apologized to Francesca for terrorizing her.

Francesca apologized, happy that I love her enough to terrorize her.

Meteorologists apologized for their predictions.

As for CNN, we're not speaking.

SWIPE ME TENDER
FRANCESCA

There are many reasons to be apprehensive about whether a dating app can deliver true love, but I won't play coy with you. What has kept me from uploading myself to Cupid's digital arrow is this: the pictures.

Perhaps I'm revealing myself to be vain, or maybe insecure, but this is real talk, #no-filter.

The prospect of choosing pictures of myself for potential dates to judge gives me a cold sweat.

First, there's the feminist objection. Aren't women objectified enough?

With most dating apps like Tinder, the written bios are short to nonexistent, and the profiles are primarily photos. Do I really want to make the online-shopping version of myself for men to select or reject with a literal flick of their fingers?

Should I include my measurements? I can be returned for store credit only.

Granted, Tinder offers equal-opportunity objectification for all genders and sexual orientations, but for women who deal with this every day IRL (Internet-speak for in real life), it's the cherry on top of a sexist sundae.

But I get it, looks are an undeniable part of sexual attraction. I'd want to check out a guy's photo, too.

So we arrive at the more mundane insecurity. I don't love pictures of me.

My self-confidence has never been based on my looks. For better or worse, almost always for worse, we form our self-image around the time we become aware of the opposite sex, during middle school and high school.

That's why we're all trembling balls of need dressed as functioning humans.

Revenge of the nerds is a fantasy for a reason. In real life, all the nerds feel like nerds forever.

When I hit puberty, I got glasses, acne, and my once-straight hair frizzed its way into nascent curls. God threw me a bone — I had naturally straight teeth — but teenage boys aren't orthodontists, so that wasn't the rocket ship to popularity you might think.

So I leaned on other strengths. I was smart and I could be funny, that was how I made friends. By the time I grew into my nose and found the good curly-hair products, my self-perception had been fixed.

I've also been told flat out I'm not photogenic. I've been told the picture of me on this very book jacket "doesn't do me justice." I think people intend this as a compliment, but social media has made the online images of ourselves the primary point of contact for friends, employers, and now, potential mates.

My best friend agrees. "Being photogenic is much better than being pretty in person."

This isn't a modern problem, it's a modern solution. Deceiving potential mates has been part of romance for centuries.

Cyrano de Bergerac could have used a good Instagram filter.

Give credit where credit is due: I know that the men on these apps aren't looking to date a photo. They're looking for a real person.

They're just judging us by our photos.

So that means they're projecting, a lot.

If a picture says a thousand words, then I need to control the narrative.

What kind of smile falls between school picture and *Sports Illustrated*? I want to be down-to-earth and natural, but I want to play the game, too.

They gotta swipe right, right?

What is tasteful girlfriend-cleavage? Asking for a friend.

I'm afraid that my average pictures won't be pretty enough, or if I post only the best pictures, I'll be disappointing in person. What if I'm not what the guy expected?

Dating apps are expectation-generating machines. They invite you to project wildly onto the person.

It's the projected version of me that I'm really afraid of. Who is she? Who is the Tinder version of me that the real me will have to compete with when I actually meet a guy? She'll be different every time, depending on the man. She's in his head, I can't control her.

But now that I'm writing this, I'm changing my mind. What am I afraid of? My silent, un-photogenic, two-dimensional self?

REQUIEM FOR A MEAL
LISA

One man's ceiling is another man's floor.

And one man's entree is another man's pet.

Today I'm talking about one of my chickens, who just died.

And yes, I had it cremated.

Rather than barbecued.

I can't decide if this makes absolute sense.

Or is completely crazy.

You be the judge.

To give you some background, I keep a flock of about fifteen hens, of different varieties. There are white Wyandottes, a shiny black Australorp, a few Rhode Island Reds, and brown Ameraucanas, which lay greenish-blue eggs.

At my house, there *is* such a thing as green eggs and ham.

Without the ham.

I've become a vegetarian, and it was the hens that turned me into one, because they're so damn cute and smart.

In other words, I used to love chicken.

But now I love chickens.

My hens are all named for Gilbert & Sullivan characters, since Daughter Francesca and I love Gilbert & Sullivan, and she performed in their musicals in college, at the Agassiz Theatre.

So our coop is named the Eggassiz Theater.

I know, I need to get a life.

The standout hens are leading ladies like Yum-Yum and Princess Ida, but the docile Plymouth Barred Rocks tend to flock together, happily clucking away, so they're collectively called the Women's Chorus.

By the way, I don't have any roosters. I'm not discriminating against men, but I don't want to live with anything that wakes up earlier than I do.

I've had the hens for eight years, and in their early days, they laid about seven or eight eggs a day total, which was awesome.

I heartily recommend having a pet who feeds you, rather than the other way around.

In those days, I had so many eggs that I handed them out to friends, brought them to New York for Francesca, or even gave them as a hostess gift.

Luckily, I have the kind of friends who

think eggs are a good gift.

I'd say my friends are good eggs.

But I'm above that sort of pun.

Anyway, my hens are getting older, and nowadays, they lay only one egg a day, if that. I'm no biologist, but I think they're in menopause.

Or henopause?

Either way, they're running out of eggs.

And so am I.

And unfortunately, the other day, one of the Women's Chorus looked like she was ailing, so we went to the chicken vet.

Yes, there is such a thing as a chicken vet. Thank God.

The vet said that my hen was basically dying of old age since eight years was elderly for a chicken, which meant that my entire flock was ready to join AARP, if not headed for that great chicken coop in the sky.

Sadly, he also said that the hen was suffering and recommended that I euthanize her, so I said yes, and she passed away peacefully.

Moment of silence.

After which I had to deal with a dead chicken.

To back up a minute, I've lost one or two other chickens, but that was a different time of the year, so I buried them in my private little pet cemetery. But this time of year, the ground is too frozen for digging, and when I mentioned that fact to the vet, he suggested that I put her in the freezer until spring.

I rejected that option.

I know a lot of people have chicken in their freezer, but I don't think it's precisely the same thing.

My other options were two. I could have her cremated and the ashes disposed of by the company, or I could have her cremated and have the ashes returned to me.

I chose the latter, because if you care enough to cremate something, you should care enough to keep the ashes.

And the ashes just arrived, in a small cardboard box, with a sympathy card that reads, "This is to certify that CHICKEN, the beloved pet of LISA SCOTTOLINE, was individually cremated."

Which made me think I should've given the hen her own name, not just a member of the Women's Chorus.

I mean, when I go, I hope my urn says more than, HUMAN.

I put her ashes in my office, which already contains one chest of horse ashes, five boxes of dog ashes, and one box of cat ashes.

It's not an office, it's a mausoleum.

And you know what?
I'm fine with that.
My animals are with me forever.
Rest in peace, little CHICKEN.

PEOPLE OF EARTH
LISA

Recently, actor Harrison Ford was in the news because he had a plane crash, which he survived with "minor trauma."

This is a news story I can't even begin to understand.

First, who walks away from a plane crash with only minor trauma?

I got minor trauma *reading* about the plane crash.

Second, Harrison Ford is such a skilled pilot that when his engine failed, he managed to crash his plane into a golf course, instead of somebody's house.

I'm betting he got a hole in one.

I give props to Harrison Ford.

Or maybe a propeller.

Third, he was flying a single-engine airplane, described as a "vintage plane from World War II." So many things about this sentence confuse me, that I don't know where to begin.

71

I'm trying to understand why anybody would want to fly a single-engine plane anywhere. I like my planes to have as many engines as possible. This way, if the first five fail, the last twenty-seven won't.

That's just common sense.

You don't have to be an airplane mechanic to have that opinion, or even be good at numbers.

You just have to know that there's something about engines that makes the plane stay parallel, and as long as you're parallel, you're not perpendicular.

It's geometry, only life or death.

In fact, if they asked me at the ticket counter if I wanted extra engines with that, I would answer, "yes, totally."

I wouldn't even mind if they didn't put the engine on the side, but just mixed it in with all the other engines.

Bottom line, when it comes to engines, more is better.

Remember that.

Then we come to another confusing thing about the sentence, which is the word "vintage."

To be clear, I love words, and "vintage" is one of my favorite. I'm fine with "vintage" when it describes wines and cars.

But not when it describes an airplane.

I'm trying to understand why anybody would want to fly a vintage airplane.

Because it was built almost seventy years ago.

Try to think of something else that was built seventy years ago that still works.

Did you get the answer yet?

Of course you didn't.

Do you know why?

The answer is nothing.

Toasters are good for six years.

Televisions are good for four.

Cell phones are good for two.

Marriages, we're talking five to seven, tops.

Just kidding.

I was talking about my marriages to Thing One and Thing Two.

Yours may last longer, depending on the mileage.

But even beyond the vintage aspect of the plane Harrison Ford was flying, I'm trying to understand why it's fun to fly around in the air, at all.

I love it here, on Earth.

Admittedly, there's things going wrong on the planet, but I generally like the way it feels underneath my feet.

Especially my bare feet.

Earth is simply the best, for foot support.

Also for jumping, running, or riding a bike.

Nothing in the air beats anything on the land, and that's why I don't get these people who want to go to Mars, either.

You may have read about them, a group of people who bought a one-way ticket to Mars, a flight which will take seven to eight months, and once they get to Mars, they will settle there, forever.

How many things are wrong with that sentence?

I stopped counting at 3,938,282,849.

Because I have better things to do.

Like walk around.

THE QUITTERS CLUB
FRANCESCA

The first almost-warm night after a long winter, I found myself on the roof of an apartment building on the Lower East Side with a group of people I didn't know very well. Two were friends of mine, but the others I had only met that night. It was still a little too cold for a roof hang, but no one would admit it. We huddled close around an electric lantern, warming ourselves with beach towels for blankets and whiskey for everything else.

The girl who lived there was our drunken leader. She started it.

"Let's go around, and everyone say something that they're proud of, or something that scared you, or whatever. Something real."

A nervous laughter spread around our circle. I zipped my jacket all the way up to my chin.

"No, seriously, don't be shy. I don't know

half you guys, so who cares? Say it, and take a drink, and pass it around. Say something real."

My friend started. She had just given her two weeks' notice at her job in marketing to pursue comedy full-time. She wasn't sure how it was all going to work out yet, but she had decided if she was going to make it in the improv comedy world, she needed more time to create, to audition, and to write.

The next guy had quit his PhD program in English literature, after completing all the requirements but his dissertation, in order to focus on running his start-up company that makes generosity more convenient, by enabling tip-jar gratuity and charitable donations via credit card.

Another had moved to New York City for a job in a company that folded two months after he arrived. But instead of moving back home, he changed career tracks, developed Plan B on the fly, and found he liked it better than Plan A anyway.

All the stories went like this. One had left a law office, to her parents' chagrin. Another had a playwriting residency that fell through.

Finally, the girl hosting shared how she had decided to quit labels and embrace the ambiguity of her attraction to men and women. She had fallen in love. And that was all that mattered.

All through school, kids are taught the mantra, "quitters never win, and winners never quit." I guess it's true that if you're quitting because you're afraid of failure, it's a mistake.

But what if you're staying because you're afraid of success? Maybe a different success, or one that takes a bit of experimenting? Or one that defies definition?

My mother always allowed me to quit. She emphasized that I had to *try,* but once I tried something, I was free to make up my mind. Sometimes, it was good that I didn't quit at the first sign of trouble. I was terrified on my first day at horseback-riding camp, but my mom told me I had to stay for three lessons to give it a fair try.

More than twenty years later, I consider horses part of my DNA.

But then, I also hated my first day of ballet lessons. The teacher was mean, and they wouldn't let me wear a tutu. Again, my mom made me stick with it for a couple of weeks.

I quit.

I have no regrets. Toe-shoes look painful as hell, and I don't need anyone's permission to wear a tutu.

When you're an adult, the stakes are raised. Quitting doesn't look great on a resume. Change brings risk. Risk costs money.

I myself was feeling particularly vulnerable at the moment. I had very recently made the decision to leave an agent with whom I had been working since I graduated college. That this agent believed in me had been the touchstone I returned to whenever self-doubt threatened to derail me. But as time passed, I began to feel that while I respected this person enormously, she wasn't the person to help me realize my vision for my career. I didn't know what I would get as an alternative, but I knew what I had didn't feel right.

After a phone conversation I had drafted and rehearsed, we parted ways on amicable terms. But I remember saying to my boyfriend at the time, "I either just made a defining decision to start my career, or I made the biggest mistake of my life."

I was terrified.

But when it was my turn to say this all out loud, I felt something else.

I was proud.

These new friends reminded me that sometimes you have to quit to create who

78

you really are. Sometimes the parameters someone else sets for you aren't the ones to build your life upon. Life's a gamble; make sure you're risking it all for the right reward.

I felt lucky to be in the company of such brave, ambitious, determined people.

Quitters who just might win.

Spanked

LISA

You can't keep a good woman down.

Or rather, in.

I'm talking, of course, about Spanx.

If you don't know what Spanx is, let me tell you.

It's a girdle.

But it's called a "body shaping garment," in that it compresses your flesh, nerves, and internal organs, so that you look thinner. In other words, Spanx is a great idea if you don't like oxygen.

Anyway, you might remember that about six years ago, I wrote about how much I hated Spanx. I got introduced to them when I bought a pair by accident, thinking they were tights. I got my size, which is B.

For Beautiful.

I took them home and put them on, which was like slipping into a tourniquet. I actually managed to squeeze myself into them, then I put on a dress and looked at myself

80

in the mirror.

From the front, I looked like a Tootsie Roll with legs.

From the back, instead of having buttocks, I had buttock.

In other words, my lower body had been transformed into a cylinder. I had become the cardboard in the roll of toilet paper. I no longer had saddlebags where God intended.

Also the elastic waistband was giving me a do-it-yourself hysterectomy.

Plus I couldn't breathe.

Actually, that's incorrect. I could inhale, but not exhale.

Turns out you need both.

Who knew?

I didn't understand the product, so I went to the website, which explained that they were "slimming apparel." The website claimed that "these innovative undergarments eliminate VBL (visible bra lines) and VPL (visible panty lines)."

Would this be a good time to say that I'm in favor of VBL and VPL? Especially VPL. In fact, I want my P as V as possible.

You know why?

Because I wear P.

I don't know what kind of signal we're sending if we want our butts to suggest otherwise.

Also, when I looked in the mirror, I noticed that the fat on my hips was being squeezed upward, leaving a roll at my waist that could pass for a flotation device.

I checked the website, and Spanx had the solution, in "slimming camis." That is, camisoles that fit like Ace bandages, which presumably grabbed the fat roll at the waist and squeezed it upward, so that it popped out at the top, as breasts.

Ta-da!

Or rather, ta-tas!

So I was cranky about my Spankies.

I threw them out and wrote about how much I hated them.

At the time, some women replied by email, agreeing with me, but most disagreed, saying they loved their Spanx.

But evidently, no more.

Or maybe they died from lack of circulation.

Today I saw an article in the newspaper, reporting that Spanx sales have taken a downturn.

I don't normally rejoice in the misfortunes of others, but YAY!

And why are sales sliding?

Because women wanted to be comfortable!

Also, their spleens staged a protest.

Because you can't keep a good woman down.

Or compressed.

We got depressed.

Because we were oppressed.

Women are learning to accept themselves, just the way we are.

Go, us!

But the same newspaper article also said that women were ditching their Spanx for yoga pants, which is like jumping out of the frying pan and into the fire.

I have a pair of yoga pants, but on me, they're yogurt pants.

And believe me, the fruit is on the bottom.

In fact, as I get older, *everything* is on the bottom.

But Spanx isn't taking this setback lying down.

Which is surprising, because if you wear Spanx, that's all you can do.

Spanx has a new president, and she's starting to stress comfort, such as bras with "soft-touch underwire contouring."

When was the last time you saw a "soft" underwire bra?

I have an underwire bra, which feels like under-barbed-wire.

I wear it for book signings, when I want to look younger.

It rides up to the middle of my breasts, leaving a red line on my skin that looks like somebody played connect the dots with my nipples.

So I won't be buying the "soft-touch" underwire.

Why?

I'm not a soft touch.

ADVICE TO A YOUNG TRADESWOMAN, WRITTEN BY AN OLD ONE
LISA

Benjamin Franklin coined the expression, "Time is money."

I'm coining a new expression — "Time is money is calories."

I know.

I'm a genius, right?

Franklin used his term in his book, *Advice to a Young Tradesman, Written by an Old One.*

I'm using my term in this book, which has a lot funnier title.

Let's be real.

Franklin may have written the Constitution, but did he ever write a book called, *I've Got Sand in All the Wrong Places*?

I don't have much in common with Ben Franklin, except that we're both from Philly and we both wear bifocals.

Though one of us *invented* bifocals.

I know, he was such a show-off.

Also I went to Penn, and he invented Penn.

But still, not my point.

Besides, he was famously single, and I am famously celibate.

Sort of the same thing.

He had illegitimate children, I have illegitimate dogs.

Anyway, I can give Franklin's maxim a modern spin, because of the epiphany I had at the end of the day, when I was lying in bed thinking about life.

I know what you're thinking.

Don't think about life at the end of the day.

At the end of the day, you're too tired to think about life. This is generally true for me. I lie in bed and am too tired to think positively. Even Shakespeare said, "sleep knits the raveled sleeve of care."

At the end of the day, my care sleeve is unraveled.

That's why the best thing to do at the end of the day is drink.

Or failing that, watch TV until you are really really tired, then quickly switch off the TV and fall right asleep. This way, you can avoid thinking about your life until it's too late to do anything about it.

And you're dead.

Too dark?

To stay on point, it was at the end of the

day, not a very good day, and frankly, I was beating myself up.

I'm the only person who beats me up, and I'm as good as any prizefighter.

I win and lose, at the same time.

Anyway, the other night, I started to think about all the things that I was supposed to get done that day, but the day had just slipped away from me. I had lost track of time.

I started to worry about money, because I was wondering if I saved enough for retirement, but I knew I hadn't. I didn't know when I would be able to retire or where all my money was going. I had lost track of my money.

And then about the same time, I was feeling fat. I had gained three pounds, and I was wondering how the hell that had happened, since it feels like I never eat anything and still I gain weight. I had lost track of my calories.

Time is money is calories.

These worries are a threesome.

No, not that kind of threesome.

I know they're not the same worries, but I can't separate them, and they're all solved basically the same way.

For example, if I had a Things To Do List, then I would be able to keep better track of my time and get more done.

And if I had kept an online budget, then I would know where my money went and I could save more.

The only way I ever lost weight was using the Lose It app, which records the calorie count of everything I eat.

So I'm going to change my ways.

Or maybe not.

Life is short.

You know what else Benjamin Franklin said?

"I wake up every morning at nine and grab for the morning paper. Then I look at the obituary page. If my name is not on it, I get up."

Truth.

How Much Is a Tracksuit?

FRANCESCA

I recently turned twenty-nine, which is the first birthday (for women) that people start consoling you over. But I wasn't bummed at all. I love cake. And I'm not afraid of getting older. I want to live forever.

I just don't want to work forever.

So this tax season, I realized I have to start saving for my retirement.

I've never been a procrastinator, but it's hard to feel like you *need* to plan for something thirty-five years in advance.

I haven't made plans for Memorial Day.

But when I started doing the math, I got scared. I don't make a lot of money, and since I've chosen to make a career telling stories, I probably never will. If I want the small amount of money I can live without to grow into enough money to live on, I need to start investing now.

Or yesterday.

Or in the womb.

I can't afford to grow into the idea that I'm going to grow old someday.

So I figure I've got about forty years of hustling until I'm seventy. By that time, I'll need to have saved enough money for, let's say, thirty more years of life.

Think living until a hundred is optimistic? You seriously underestimate how much kale I eat.

When I graduated college, my mom gave me a book by Suze Orman called *The Money Book for the Young, Fabulous, and Broke,* and while the title was right on the money, there was one problem: it was published in 2007.

Before the economy hit the fan.

The advice was geared toward people working at traditional companies that provide retirement plans and employer-matching 401(k)s.

Do those jobs exist anymore? And are they hiring?

Most of my friends are self-employed or juggling one dream career while working part-time elsewhere — in short, no benefits.

Social Security will be long extinct by the time my generation goes gray. And unless *Jurassic Park 4* is about finding pension-DNA stuck in tree sap, it's not coming back.

National debt finds a way.

Why doesn't anyone tell us how to do this? I went to Harvard, yet the entirety of my finance knowledge came from Kristen Wiig's *SNL* impression of Suze Orman and Google.

Is everybody my age secretly socking away cash and not telling me?

FOMO is Fear Of Missing Out. I have FORO.

Fear Of Running Out.

So I said farewell to youth and embraced retirement planning. I was so proud of myself for figuring out that I need an IRA, I didn't realize that was only step one. I still had to choose between a Roth IRA, a traditional IRA, a SEP IRA, and probably others I'm supposed to know but don't.

They all shelter your investment from taxes but prevent you from withdrawing your money until you're fifty-nine-and-a-half.

I thought we stopped counting halves after age nine.

The IRS is so immature.

But there are all these minute differences about who can contribute to what, and which ones lower your taxable income, etc. For example, a Roth IRA allows you to withdraw money early to buy your first house.

Whereas a traditional IRA would prefer you wait until marriage.

When I opened my IRA, the bank associate asked me how much I'd like to contribute. I'd done my homework, and I knew the annual limit for people like me was pretty low, so I told her I'd like to put away the maximum I'm allowed.

"Okay. But I can't tell you what that is." She smiled.

"You don't know?"

"Well, I'm not allowed to tell you. You'd have to ask your accountant."

Why is everything tax-related cloaked in secrecy? The IRS is this Oz-like master, with questionably corrupt forces at the top getting all the benefits, while the rest of us pay lots of money for purposes unknown, but we obey, because we're too confused by all the categories and acronyms and pages upon pages of rules, rules that if anyone actually read, would make absolutely no sense.

Is this the federal tax code or Scientology?

In either case, I don't want to get audited.

But I did it! I successfully started saving for my retirement. This calls for cake!

I can only lick the icing now, but in thirty-and-a-half years, I can eat a whole piece.

DOGGIE DRAMZ

LISA

I can't figure my dogs out.

It may be they're smarter than I am.

In which case, they'd better be able to write a book, because that's what pays the bills around here.

My latest dog drama concerns something that should be simple.

Food.

In fact, if I were going to pick two areas in which I would consider myself generally knowledgeable, it would be dogs or food. But evidently, when dogs and food are put together, I'm stumped.

To give you some background, I've had dogs my entire life: mutts, rescue dogs, purebreds, all kinds of dogs. And all of these dogs reacted exactly the same way when there was a bowl of food put in front of them.

They gobbled it up instantly.

The only problem I've ever had with dogs

Ruby is just happy she is not the one causing trouble.

at mealtime is that when I've had more than one dog, I feed them in separate places, so they don't get aggressive.

Still, in the past, this has not been a problem. I have crates for all my dogs, and I feed them in their crates, which makes them love their crates the way I love my kitchen.

Because it's delicious.

So what's happening is that I have Ruby The Crazy Corgi, who eats reliably, like a normal dog. I put her in her cage and give her a bowl of kibble, and she wolfs it right down.

That is, if wolves had four-inch legs.

Ruby is not the problem, for once. She's reveling in the fact that the others are getting in trouble this time.

Because the four Cavalier King Charles spaniels — Little Tony, Peach, Boone, and Kit — are as fussy about eating as the name of their breed. And the weird thing is, they're not fussy about what they eat, they're fussy about the way they eat it.

Don't think I'm being a control freak, because you know me better than that.

But here's what happens every morning: I put a full bowl of kibble in the cage of each of the Cavaliers and I close the door of the cage.

They don't eat, but for the next hour, they proceed to stare at the bowl.

Then, when I go to open the cage door and pick up the bowl of food, they start eating.

When I put the bowl back down and close the door, they stop eating.

This was driving me crazy, because I was spending my entire morning opening and closing crate doors and watching to see if they'd eat. And then I started experimenting, so I would take some of the kibble out of the bowls and dump it on the crate pad.

Which is when I noticed that Kit would

eat the food only if it were on the crate pad.

And Boone would eat the food only if his cage door was open, but not if it was closed.

So now I have four Cavaliers with four different modes of eating, and I don't understand this behavior at all.

I know you're thinking that I should just take the food away, and that's what I do. When I've spent about an hour dumping kibble onto crate pads and picking it up again, or opening and closing crate doors, or lifting food bowls and putting them back down again, I finally give up.

I collect all four bowls and put them in the refrigerator.

I vow I won't offer any food again until the next day.

I say to myself, if those crazy dogs are hungry enough, they'll eat.

And sometimes, that works.

But still, I'm too much of an Italian mother to let anything miss a meal.

And I worry about it all morning, in the back of my mind, when I'm working.

And I would really like to understand this behavior.

I don't need this degree of doggie drama.

Is anybody out there smarter than my dogs?

MOMMY'S DAY OUT
FRANCESCA

The last time my mom came to visit, I lost her.

It was like that movie *Baby's Day Out,* except with my parent. I turned my back for one second, and the little rascal got away from me.

I imagined her crawling along an I-beam at some high-rise construction site.

But she's afraid of heights, so more likely she'd be in Times Square, telling The Naked Cowboy he isn't dressed warmly enough.

It started with tickets to see the new Larry David play. My mom checked that she had the tickets for the third or fourth time.

"It says, 'late arrivals will not be seated,' " she read, for my benefit. My mom is early to everything. We left with an hour to spare.

And yet, we found ourselves in a cab crawling up Sixth Avenue for a half hour with fifteen blocks to go. I checked our route on my smartphone; the driving esti-

She's in there somewhere.

mate to get to the theater was fifteen minutes, the walking was only ten.

"I think we should get out," I said.

"Really?" My mom looked aghast.

"Yeah, we're close, but this traffic is going to take forever."

But I'd inadvertently hit the panic button in my mom's ever-punctual brain. She swiped, tapped, and banged her credit card on the automated reader before throwing it at me in anguish ("Mom, it's a touch screen now, we've been over this . . ."), and she couldn't wait for the cabbie to pull over before she shot out of the taxi.

I scurried after her. "Wait, we have time, we don't have to run."

But she was already jogging down the crowded sidewalk, dodging men with briefcases and women wearing pantyhose with sneakers.

I awkwardly half-ran after her, not eager to claim the crazy woman sprinting in front of me as my own, but not wanting to lose sight of her bobbing blond head either.

My mom turned back only occasionally to furiously mouth the words, "COME ON!" and "WHY AREN'T YOU RUNNING?"

This made me laugh, which only made her angrier.

I was only a few yards behind her until a major intersection, when she darted out against the light. I winced as she put her hands up to the hoods of honking cars like an action-movie star.

Thankfully, even Manhattan drivers won't mess with my mother.

So she was a good ten yards ahead of me when she got to one corner and pointed west, mouthing, "This way?"

The theater was on 48th Street between Sixth and Seventh Avenues. We were on Sixth, so we were less than a block away — with plenty of time, I might add.

I nodded.

She bolted left. I figured I'd catch up to her in a minute.

Until I reached the corner and looked up. The sign read 49th Street.

I was so busy chasing her, I didn't realize we'd overshot it by a block. But by now, the blond head had vanished.

I called my mom's cell phone — no answer.

I called again. Surely, she would pick up, once she didn't immediately see the theater where it should be.

It went to voice mail.

I called a third time. SURELY, she would at least LOOK at her phone, once she realized her daughter was no longer behind her.

Nope.

I ran all the way down 49th Street looking for her. I stopped at the corner of Broadway, at a complete loss as to which way she'd gone.

Ten minutes to curtain. I headed to the theater, praying she'd be there waiting.

She wasn't.

I called her again, and this time, she answered. Like any parent who'd been through a scare, my relief curdled instantly to anger. "Where are you?!" I screamed.

"I don't know!" she yelled.

"How do you not know? It's a grid!"

We both calmed down, and I coached her to find me. When she arrived, her hair was frizzed with sweat. She looked so cute, I couldn't be mad.

We rushed inside. The usher pointed us to our seats, and a concession worker walked by. My mom asked me to buy her a water.

"Sorry, we're out. I only have wine," he said.

"Fine."

He handed it to me in a plastic sippy cup.

I gave Mommy her juice just as the houselights dimmed, and I collapsed into my seat.

Next time, I'm bringing a nanny.

CELEBRITY CRUSHED
LISA

It's important for you to know that I'm a human being subject to the same foibles that other human beings are.

Specifically, I get celebrity crushes.

My first real celebrity crush was George Clooney, and you and I may have that in common.

I had a crush on him because I thought he was funny, smart, and liked smart and funny women, and I was proven correct when he married a lawyer.

Just not this lawyer.

(Me.)

Of course the lawyer that George Clooney married was almost twenty years his junior, but we have all come to learn that the dating ground for single men is decades-younger women, even if that means they have to help them with their French homework.

In fact, especially if that means they have

to help them with their French homework.

But the thing about a celebrity crush is that it isn't realistic.

It's fantasy.

That's probably why its object is a movie actor, in other words, somebody who acts crushworthy for a living.

They could secretly be a jerk, but just a terrific actor.

After George Clooney got married, I knew I had to move on, because I would never date a married man, even in my dreams.

I immediately latched on to Bradley Cooper because I thought he was funny, smart, and he liked funny and smart women.

So you see the pattern.

Guess who thinks she's funny and smart?

(Me.)

(Rather, I.)

Bradley Cooper, however, started dating a model who was roughly twenty years his junior, then moved on to another model who was twenty years his junior, but as he is not yet married, he remains my celebrity crush.

Also alternative babysitter.

But I have a secret celebrity crush, one I've never written about because I didn't re-alize it until recently, when I watched my umpteenth episode of *Seinfeld.*

But my crush isn't Jerry Seinfeld.

The more I watched *Seinfeld,* the more I realized that the writing is what turned me on.

Because I'm a writer!

And the writer was Larry David.

I know, purists will say that Jerry Seinfeld wrote, too, but Jerry Seinfeld is already married and you know my rule about that.

But Larry David recently became unmarried.

So fast-forward to me visiting Francesca in New York, and we have nothing to do for the night and I say, "Hey, why don't we get tickets to that new Larry David play, which will be funny and smart?"

Unsuspecting, she agrees.

Francesca just told you the story about how we got to the theater, but I want to focus on what happens after the end of the play, when, as luck would have it, Larry David and Rita Wilson come out on the stage, as themselves, and announce that they are holding a fundraiser for Broadway Cares, which is a charity run by actors to benefit people with AIDS.

Go on, I think to myself, listening with interest.

Typical of Larry to have such a big heart.

Or so I fantasize.

So then Rita Wilson announces that any-body who is willing to donate to this charity will get to meet her and Larry David and have a picture taken with them.

I can't believe my ears.

It's embarrassing to admit, but I jumped at the chance, raising my hand.

Francesca looked over, bewildered. "Mom, what are you doing?"

"Giving to charity, of course," I told her, because no mother tells her daughter the absolute truth, especially when the mother is about to make a complete fool of herself.

"Do you realize this is an auction?" she said, gesturing at the crowd.

Which was when I realized that bidding was going on, and all of the hands were going down, but my hand was still up.

I say this as an excuse, but the truth is, I would've bid anyway.

Because the next thing that happened was that Rita Wilson pointed at me and said, "Sold!"

For $2,000.

"Mom?" Francesca's face went white. "Really?"

Now, look, I know that's a lot of money, but it was for a good cause, which was me meeting Larry David.

Anyway, we jumped out of our seats, hustled down the aisle, and joined a line of people, all of whom were willing to spend $2,000 because they had a crush on Larry David.

Not really; all of them were married couples from New Jersey.

I was the only single woman, if you don't count Francesca, who has no romantic interest in Larry David. But if she did, I would knock her down and step over her body to get to him.

My first thought was, I didn't look good enough to meet my celebrity crush. I hadn't showered or blown out my hair because the evening had been so last-minute, and I was wearing my glasses, not my contacts.

Between us, there's not much difference in me either way, but for some reason I'm more confident in my contacts.

Nobody has to know they're multifocal, which are contacts for old people.

And anyway, I told myself, Larry David is pretty old.

Plus he wore glasses, so maybe he liked women who wore glasses.

But for one problem.

Guess what I wasn't wearing?

A bra.

Can you imagine?

I had on a big sweater, and since I didn't realize I was going to meet my crush, I hadn't bothered finding my push-up, which is bound to the bottom of my underwear drawer by cobwebs.

To state the obvious, braless isn't a good look for a woman my age.

Especially one trying to catch Larry David as her next ex-husband.

Thing Three!

Anyway, so we neared the head of the line, and my mouth went completely dry.

I could spot Larry David because he was so tall and he looked smart, funny, and vaguely uncomfortable as all the couples pumped his hand and told him how much they loved *Seinfeld*.

As the line inched forward, I tried to think of something smart and funny to say, but I was too nervous. I kept my coat wrapped around me, to hide the effects of gravity, and I even put Francesca in front of me because I was such a chicken.

It's one thing to have a celebrity crush.

And another to actually meet him.

I considered running away until they took my credit card, and the next thing I knew, we were at the head of the line.

Rita Wilson was standing ahead of Larry David, greeting everyone, because she was clearly the warmest and nicest person ever, and she gave Francesca a big hug and thanked us for giving to such an "important charity."

I kept my secret to myself.

Then Francesca shook Larry David's hand, apparently unaware of his animal magnetism, and she told him how much she liked *Seinfeld.*

He nodded politely and said, "Thanks."

What a guy!

At which point I was engulfed in a Rita Wilson hug, and I hugged her back, just for comfort's sake.

She smelled great.

I was almost too nervous to let her go.

But I did, and then I was face-to-face with my celebrity crush, who smiled, stuck out his hand, and said, "Pleased to meet you."

I hesitate to tell you what I said to him.

Because it is so completely pathetic.

But this is a book in which we promised you the emotional and/or the literal truth, so here goes:

I said, "Hi, I really love your writing and I'm single."

Then I blinked.

Because even I could not believe I said such a thing.

Francesca whirled around, her mouth

I'll never wash that shoulder again.

dropping open.

Rita Wilson smiled nervously. I know she considered calling security, but she didn't. She just laughed.

And as for Thing Three, he leaned over with a slight frown and asked, "Pardon me?"

Now, dear reader, I can only assume that he did this because he was saving me from myself. Or maybe he just didn't hear.

But whatever the reason, it gave me a choice:

I could repeat my embarrassment.

Or I could just get back with Bradley Cooper.

(I stay flexible on my celebrity crushes.)

But I'm happy to report that this story has a happy ending, because I answered:

"I said, 'I'm pleased to meet you.' " And then I added, "And thank you for donating your time for such a worthy cause."

"I'm happy to do it," Larry David said with a pleasant smile, at which point Rita Wilson stepped in and arranged us for a photograph, which someone else took.

Guess what?

Larry put his arm around me for the photo.

!!!!!!!

Luckily, my middle-aged breasts were hidden inside my coat.

And my dignity was restored.

Until now.

THIS IS THE PITS
LISA

Just when you think women's health isn't getting enough attention, along comes good news.

Whew!

I'm talking about a new medical procedure developed to address one of our most pressing female problems:

Sweat.

Yes, we sweat.

And something needs to be done about it, evidently.

You may have seen the news story, which reports a great advance in scientific knowledge for women. A machine has been invented that will microwave your underarms and thus eliminate sweating and underarm hair.

So much about this is wonderful that I don't know where to start.

I guess with the microwave part, because I love my microwave and I'm always looking for new things to microwave. I hadn't thought to look under my own arms, but you learn something new every day.

This news is especially welcome in the summer months, when it's hot and we're microwaving instead of cooking.

Nobody wants to slave over a hot oven in August.

By the way, we both know that August is a total excuse.

Nobody wants to slave over a hot oven in December, either, but let's keep that secret.

Just play along.

They'll never know.

If you end up having to slave over a hot oven in August, then you can be a real martyr and give everybody guilt.

Don't miss the opportunity to Be a Martyr/Give Guilt.

This is how you teach people your True Value.

Of course, if you microwave your armpit, you won't have to sweat in August.

Or, ever.

The way armpit-microwaving works is that the machine concentrates energy on the sweat glands and hair follicles in the under-arm area, creating such intense heat that it destroys the glands and follicles entirely, so they don't regenerate.

Now *there's* a good idea.

If this sounds like a brush fire in your armpit, it might as well be.

The side effects are pain and swelling.

Also screaming at the top of your lungs.

They say this procedure is "noninvasive."

I beg to differ.

If I lift up my arm and you torch my glands, that would be the very definition of "invasive."

That might even be "criminal."

In a related story, I read about hospitals in New York that are having hairstylists come to maternity wards and blow-dry the hair of the new moms, who want to look pretty for their Facebook, Instagram, and Twitter pictures.

Another great idea.

I think it's extremely important for women to look their best at all times, and fifteen hours of painful labor is no excuse.

Not to mention nine months before that, of growing another human being inside your very body.

It's only the miracle of life.

Stop slacking.

In fact, if pregnant women microwaved their armpits before they entered the hospital to give birth, then they wouldn't sweat even during labor.

Clearly, somebody's thinking around here. Plan ahead, ladies.

One stylist who fixed a new mom's hair in the hospital explains that women want their hair to look spruced up, but not fussy.

I think that's because the baby's supposed to be fussy, not the mother.

The stylist said that new moms don't want "black-tie-event hair."

That makes sense.

After labor, the only thing I wanted tied was my tubes.

The news story reported that a hospital-room booking with a stylist from an upscale salon can cost as much as $700.

I can't think of a better use for the money, the day your baby is born.

College funds can wait.

The only way to improve this idea is to have the hairstylist blow-dry the infant's hair, too.

Nobody's hair looks worse than on the day they're born.

Babies don't have bed head, they have birth-canal head.

It's not pretty, and infants need to learn the importance of pretty from day one.

You never get a second chance to make a first impression.

Especially if it's your very very *first* impression.

Of course, both of these major developments in women's health came about not because hospitals or government wanted them, but because women want them.

We have met the enemy and it is us.

We haven't gotten the message that our True Value has nothing to do with the way we look.

It has to do with how many people we make feel guilty.

Judge Doorman

FRANCESCA

Manhattan doormen are famous for being completely discreet and nonjudgmental. Somebody just needs to tell mine that.

My doorman is totally judgmental. He's the most opinionated man I've ever met, and he never holds fire. He's a macho Dominican man who can throw drag-queen levels of shade.

And I love him.

You know how everyone needs that friend who tells it to you straight? He's mine.

My closest girlfriends don't tell me the truth. They flatter me and build me up, and I like that about them. Female friendship is based upon voicing your fears and insecurities and having someone to go, "SHUT. UP. You are so perfect."

My doorman provides balance. He works the day shift, so he sees me first thing in the morning when I walk my dog. If I get any less than eight hours of sleep or skip the

116

mascara, I hear:

"You look tired, Princess."

And yes, he calls me "Princess." And "mi corazón." And "my dear."

These pet names help soften the blow when he says something like he did last week: "I don't see you in your gym clothes anymore."

"I'm going at night!" I lied.

But the next morning, I got my butt to the gym. He keeps me accountable. And he was a pretty great cheerleader last year when I was trying to shape up.

He also gives unsolicited fashion advice.

"I don't like that coat."

"I just bought this coat!" It was a camel-colored wrap coat that I had finally splurged on after obsessing over it for a month, trying on six different versions of it in various stores, and texting dressing-room selfies to my mom and best friend.

He shrugged. "Mmm, I don't like it. It's too big for you."

"It's oversized and slouchy, that's the *look.*"

"You don't need to hide in a big coat. You lost weight since the summer."

Guilting me about the gym had paid off.

But I still think my coat is chic and have defiantly worn it all autumn. But I'd be lying if I said I don't tie it a little tighter at the waist.

Sometimes I seek out his opinion — why, I don't know. Last month, I bought a watch online for my best guy friend's thirtieth birthday. I was so excited when my doorman told me it had arrived, I opened it up right there in the lobby to show him.

"What do you think, pretty nice, huh?"

"Gold?" He furrowed his brow.

"Yeah, well, in color."

"I prefer silver watches. It's more masculine. But if he likes gold . . ."

I snatched it back. Luckily, when I presented the watch to my friend, he did like gold. At least, I think he was telling me the truth.

When it comes to my love life, my doorman is the wise-cracking, overprotective father I never had. He sizes up every guy I bring by, and although my doorman is as inscrutable as the Sphinx to their faces, behind their backs, he gets catty.

When I dated a European: "Can he take you out in those tight pants?"

When I dated a quiet guy: "Does he talk?"

When I dated a short guy: "Pick on someone your own size!"

But despite my doorman's expertise in snap judgment, he's surprisingly perceptive

118

when it comes to the heavy stuff. When my last long-term relationship started to sour, he noticed it almost before I did.

"You all right? You don't seem happy. Make sure he makes you happy."

The morning after we broke up, when my eyes were puffy from crying, he glanced at me and shook his head. "Say the word, Princess, I'll kick his ass."

It made me laugh.

Because whether I agree with him all the time or not, it's nice to know that someone has your back.

My mom and my doorman are best buds, because she gets the warm, funny version of him that I see every day, and they're both no-nonsense when it comes to keeping me safe. So I often relay his one-liners to her over the phone.

When she came to visit shortly after my breakup, she had a private chat with him.

"You know," my mom said, leaning over the front desk, "I didn't think that last boyfriend was right for her, either."

She told me he replied only, "I'm sorry, ma'am. I don't comment on the personal lives of our tenants."

GOT LIMES?

LISA

You may have seen the news story that one of the major big-box stores has applied for a liquor license, which would allow consumption-on-premises.

In other words, you could drink while you shop.

Yay!

Happy days are here again!

Reportedly, the store is doing this because it's expanding its grocery and food items, but I don't care why.

Bottom's up!

I already love shopping in big-box stores.

Why?

Everything is BIG!

If you need to buy laundry detergent, the smallest bottle is 187 ounces.

And that's concentrated, so it's the equivalent of an entire ocean of laundry detergent.

That's why I buy All laundry detergent.

Because it's ALL.

In fact, you will die before you run out of laundry detergent, and you can bequeath it to your children. So after you have given your all, you can give them your All.

If you buy a can of coffee, it will be shrink-wrapped with forty-seven hundred other cans of coffee. You'll have more caffeine than you'll ever need and you can share some with your neighbors, so your entire block will be highly productive.

Or start a war.

I also buy multicolored gummy vitamins in a big-box store, and I now have 32,029,348 vitamins. If I took them all, I would gain a superpower.

Or grow a third breast covered with rainbows.

Which might be the same thing.

But you get the idea, the bottom line in big-box stores is that everything is big, plentiful, excessive, and way out of proportion.

Ain't it great?

The shopping carts are humongous, too, perfectly in scale with the massive stores, so that between the immensity of the space, the gargantuan shopping carts, and the over-the-top quantity of each item, when you step inside the store, you're a Lilliputian stepped into Brobdingnag, which is the land where the giants lived in *Gulliver's Travels.*

You probably knew that.

But I had to look it up.

Impressed?

Anyway it's a good analogy, because that's pretty much exactly how I feel when I'm pushing around one of those big carts, and like you, I go into the big-box store for one item and leave with several hundred.

In fact, I have been known to leave the store with two full carts, which shows you that Lilliputians love to shop.

Now that big-box stores will allow you to drink while you shop, I'm imagining myself walking those glistening, extra-wide aisles behind my cart-as-big-as-a-house, a Lilliputian sipping Lambrusco.

I don't have that many inhibitions to start with, and for me, liquor only makes things worse.

Or better.

I buy too much in the big-box store when I'm sober, but if I shop while I'm drinking, I'll shop until I drop.

Or until I drip.

Or both.

I might buy EVERYTHING.

Whether you think drinking-while-you-shop is a good thing depends on whether you're the massive corporation that owns the big-box stores or my retirement fund.

Either way, I'm in.

It certainly improves people's attitudes about running their errands on the weekends, if they can do them beer in hand.

It changes your Things To Do list into a Things to Drink list.

I'm wondering if the shopping carts will have cupholders in the shape of wineglasses or maybe tiny ones small enough to hold a shot glass.

Shot! Shot! Shot!

Shop! Shop! Shop!

But what happens when people start drinking while they're driving those scooters in the store?

I foresee major collisions.

It brings a whole new meaning to, "Pick up in aisle four."

Employees will come with a broom.

And a Breathalyzer.

I Saw the Sign

LISA

We're coming up on the anniversary of Mother Mary's passing.

But this isn't going to be sad.

Nobody hated sob stories more than Mother Mary.

You know her well enough to agree, if you've read the stories that Francesca and I have been writing about her for the past six years, in the newspaper and our books.

You may even have met her, if you came to one of our signings, where she was happy to monopolize the microphone.

I was delighted to have her at signings, because she did a hell of a job.

Also the price was right.

She told every family secret there was to tell, and when she ran out, she made them up.

In other words, it's in my DNA to write fiction.

She also dressed better than Francesca

and me, standing out in her lab coat like a geriatric Doogie Howser.

She often brought her backscratcher to the signings and hit me with it, for effect. Otherwise she used it to scratch her back in front of the crowd.

We Scottolines don't always confine our personal grooming to the house.

I could go on and on, saying things I remember about her, and those of you who have lost family members could do the same, about your loved ones who are no longer with us, in a physical sense.

You don't need me to tell you that they are always with us, in spirit.

And in fact, what's great to remember about Mother Mary *is* her spirit.

I always loved the story about the time I made her fly north to avoid a major hurricane heading for Florida. When she got off the plane, she was approached by a reporter who was interviewing people about the hurricane. The reporter came up to her, asking, "Did you come north because you're afraid of the hurricane?"

Mother Mary replied, "I'm not afraid of a hurricane. I *am* a hurricane."

This story is especially relevant because of something I've noticed in the time since she's been gone.

Because I think she sent me a sign.

Have you seen a sign?

I've talked to my friends who have lost family members, and many of them think that their family member has sent them a sign from beyond, or wherever we go when we're not hanging around the kitchen anymore, standing in front of the refrigerator looking for something to eat.

One of my friends says that when she sees a monarch butterfly, she knows it's a sign from her late mother, who loved monarch butterflies. Another friend of mine thinks that a double rainbow is a sign from her late father, who loved double rainbows.

Even famous people see signs.

I heard Paul McCartney give an interview, wherein he said that after he lost his beloved wife Linda, he sat on a hill at night and asked for a sign from her about whether he should remarry. An owl hooted, and Paul decided that it was the go-ahead, so he married Heather Mills.

Whom he later divorced at a cost of $48 million.

After the Paul McCartney story, I started to be skeptical about signs from the departed.

I mean, come on, Paul.

Owls hoot at night.

But here's the sign I think I got from Mother Mary, and you tell me if I'm crazy.

Because it's a sign that only she could send.

Let's go back for a moment, to the day of her memorial service, which was very sad. It was a small and tasteful ceremony, but everybody was predictably teary, and that day, it was raining.

In fact, it was raining very hard.

It was raining almost hurricane-hard.

And after the service, we came home to my house, and it had rained so hard that my entrance hall was flooded.

I'm not talking about one or two inches of water.

I'm talking about four inches of water, so much that wet rugs had to be removed and you had to wade through it to get to the front door.

The water had evidently come in under the front door of the entrance hall, but that had never happened before.

And dear reader, it never happened again.

In fact, it hasn't happened in the entire time, since the day of her funeral.

Recall that since, we've experienced very hard rains, very hard snows, and sometimes a little of both.

At the same time.

In other words, there's been major weather.

But my entrance hall never flooded again.

Not even a drop.

And so I think it's a sign.

Mother Mary wasn't the type to send butterflies, rainbows, or hoot owls.

Hurricane Mary sent a hurricane.

And so we wouldn't miss it, she put it in front of the front door.

That was Mother Mary.

She was a force of nature.

And she still is, eternally.

Now I'm a believer.

Love you, Mom.

You owe me a rug.

INCIDENT REPORT
FRANCESCA

This book is meant to be fun, but it's also about life's real moments, light and dark. This summer included one of the darkest experiences of my life, when I was assaulted and mugged. The events of that night and their repercussions were difficult to process. I've learned that trauma has to metabolize and be absorbed into your emotional system. My recovery has been full of contradictions, revealed in stages through time and self-reflection. So, I think the only accurate way for me to write about it is in pieces.

This piece is about what happened that night, the way I see it when my mind replays it, and it replays it often, with some moments in great sensory detail and other moments of infuriating blackness. If you are upset by violent crime, you may wish to skip this chapter.

After something bad happens, it's deceptively easy to retrace your decisions and wish you had made them differently. I wish I had left the party early with my friend who had a cold. I wish I had taken a cab home like I had intended. I wish I had asked one of the two guy friends I had ridden the subway with to walk me to my door instead of only accompanying me to my stop. I wish I had turned down any other street but that one.

But none of these choices were mistakes or imprudent in their own right. They were just the choices I made before someone hurt me.

I remember the rain splashing on the top steps of the Christopher Street subway stop as I emerged a little after 1 A.M., and wishing I had insisted my friends share a cab because this rain would ruin my new leather moccasins.

I hurried down the sidewalk on the balls of my feet, jumping over puddles and the rivulets of rainwater flowing toward the gutters.

I remember seeing a rat but not startling, and thinking that was brave of me.

I am not a girl easily frightened.

I had no idea that was to be tested at the very next turn.

I took a left down the street that I live on, two short blocks from home. I had my umbrella open, a thin shield of pink blocking my peripheral vision. But maybe I wouldn't have seen him anyway.

I felt a body slam into mine and an arm pull across my neck. We collapsed together on the ground, my back flat on the sidewalk. Somehow my head didn't hit the concrete, I guess because he was choking me from behind.

There was no thought but the primal knowledge that I had to get off my back. I used all my adrenaline to somehow break from his grasp and hurl myself forward onto my hands and knees.

I started to crawl away, the sensation of freedom gave me hope, but he was back on me before I had crossed a sidewalk square. He swarmed me with his body, I felt his arms all over me like an octopus, and I knelt in the tightest ball to protect myself, all the while screaming as loud as I possibly could.

I surprised myself with my own volume. I told myself I only had to resist long enough before someone came to help. But as the seconds ticked by in my brain, I realized waiting was not a survival strategy.

He got hold of me and tried to pull me toward the street. Feeling my bare knees scraping even an inch shot panic through me — I could not let him move me anywhere, least of all toward a car.

I threw my arms out onto the sidewalk, straining at one point for the small fence around a tree but unable to reach it, instead digging my fingernails into the sidewalk. I believed my life depended on my ability to stay exactly where I was.

He stopped pulling me, and again, I experienced a split second of relief — another tiny victory my spirit clung to so that I would keep fighting — before he kicked me under my chin. The impact under my jaw came as a shock. The shock made me slow to interpret the next sensation: a chain pulling taut around my waist.

My purse.

My purse?

My purse!

True elation as I realized I had a bargaining chip, something my attacker wanted that I was actually willing to give.

But it was a cross-body bag, now somewhere near the ground, tangled around my limbs, not readily coming loose when he yanked on it. He must have thought I was resisting, or maybe he was driven mad with frustration, or anger, or fear. I can only speculate as to his emotion that made the violence escalate.

Because before I could do anything, he

started hitting me, hard. I think with his fists, I'm not sure. But he hit me again and again and again. Pummeled is a better word. On my head and neck and shoulders, but the most on my head. My skull rattled with every blow, whipping my cervical spine, crushing my tongue between my teeth.

Another clear thought materialized in my battered brain:

You have to figure out a way to make this stop fast, or one of these blows will cave your head in.

I had been protecting my face with my hands as much as I could, but I realized that finding the bag was my only chance for getting rid of him. I lowered my hands to feel for the purse chain. This was when he got his best shots in.

He hit me square on my right brow. Light exploded behind my squeezed-shut eyes.

Keep feeling for it.

Again, under my right eye, snapping my head to the left.

I felt the cool metal, closed my fist around it, but now I had to lift it over my head.

Again, in the center of my forehead, hard enough to send my head ricocheting backwards on my neck, hopefully hard enough to hurt his hand.

But I'd done it. I got the chain over my

head and shoved the bag in his direction.

He bolted one way and I scrambled to my feet and ran the other. I didn't dare look over my shoulder until I was halfway down the street. By the time I turned around, he had disappeared.

My glasses were long gone, and the world was a bleary mess of dark shadows and orange streetlight. The relief of the attack being over hadn't hit me yet. Instead, the fear that I'd suppressed in order to survive came crashing over me at once.

I screamed a final time and the sound echoed down the street, ringing in my ears as if it weren't coming from my own body.

She sounded terrified and fierce.

LAUGH AT MY PAIN
FRANCESCA

They say that tragedy plus time equals comedy. But the night I was assaulted, I found, through virtue of shock, divine intervention, or head trauma, I was able to appreciate the humor in a terrible situation while it was happening.

Well, not when the assault itself was happening. That wasn't that funny. So let's skip that part:

[Intermission music while a bad thing happens.]

Fast-forward to my attacker running away with my bag and me screaming loud enough to make people living in thirteen-million-dollar town houses feel like they need more gentrification.

A group of about six young people heard me and came running to help. A blond woman led the pack. "We heard you, are you okay? What happened?"

"I'm fine, I'm fine," I said.

In retrospect, a pretty inaccurate self-assessment. But when you think you might die, and then you end up not dead, anything short of a gunshot wound is "fine."

I told them what happened, that I needed help finding my glasses, and I needed someone to call the police. They were incredibly helpful, somehow finding my glasses in the wet leaves. I put them on my face.

The world looked dirty, squashed, and very crooked, but that seemed appropriate.

"My friend is calling 911 now. Do you want to use my phone to call someone else, maybe your mom?"

"No way," I answered. "I have to calm down first."

While we waited, the blond girl introduced herself, which was so nice and normal, it actually did calm me down. Then she asked something very sweet: "Can I give you a hug?"

Boy, did I need one. The girl's name was Natalie. I only wish I had gotten her last name so I could find her and thank her.

In the next minute, the police car pulled up. The officer rolled down the window and shouted, "Get in the back, we're going to look for him!"

I hopped in like an obedient dog.

I had never been in the back of a police vehicle before. My first thought, for real?

There's not a lot of knee room.

I'm only five-five, and I winced as my bloody knees knocked the partition on every turn.

Seriously, tall people, rethink a life of crime. It's very uncomfortable.

One of the officers turned around and said, "Now I know this is difficult, but I want you to look out the window and see if you see the guy who did this."

I tried to look out the window, but it was streaked with rainwater. I pushed the button to lower it, and nothing happened. I jammed my finger in it a few more times.

Oh, duh, I thought. *The back windows are locked.*

To keep those criminal children from hurting themselves.

Rainwater aside, the main issue with finding the perp was that I hardly caught a glimpse of him. He came up behind me, knocked off my glasses, and pummeled my face in, so you know, not ideal eyewitness conditions. I told the officer as much.

"Just look for a guy holding your purse!"

My brain provided the amusing image of a thug strolling along with my fashionable tan handbag.

Reality has no such sense of humor.

After several fruitless tours around the surrounding blocks, we circled back to the street where it happened, so that I could try to give them an exact address of the crime site. And then I realized . . .

This happened right outside of the *Sex and the City* house — the brownstone HBO used for exteriors of Carrie Bradshaw's apartment!

As a fan, my emotions were mixed.

When Carrie was mugged in Season 3 of *SATC,* the criminal stole her shoes.

I was wearing cute shoes, and he didn't even notice.

We gave up on finding the guy and they drove me to the police station to "take my statement" or do whatever official crime-victim stuff they skip over on *Law & Order.*

As soon as we walked in, one of the police-men with me, Officer Green, piped up. "You know, you should cancel your credit cards."

I was shivering, bleeding, and soaking wet — canceling my cards was low on my priority list. "Um, okay, but I don't have my phone or my account number or anything."

He asked me what bank it was with and I told him.

Meanwhile, the other, Officer Moon, gave me a form to record everything that was stolen and its value. My hand was shaking so badly, I could barely hold the pen. He gently walked me through each question, holding a finger down on the line like an elementary-school teacher.

On the first item, I wrote "purse." Next to that it read, "Model," which my concussed brain failed to compute. I looked helplessly at Officer Moon.

"Brand," Moon translated.

I nodded and wrote "Gucci."

New item: Wallet. Model: Gucci.

Officer Green peered over my shoulder. "You're a Gucci girl, eh?"

"Yes, they were gifts," I said. "Up until tonight, my life was very good."

He chuckled and handed me his own cell phone. "I got your bank on the line. You just have to tell 'em your social and they can cancel the card."

I thought it was so nice of him to call them for me. I hate customer-service trees almost as much as I hate getting mugged. I thanked him and gave the info to the representative.

Then I was introduced to two detectives who asked all the same questions the police had. The detectives were perfectly nice and professional, but the process of being asked the same questions several times, to someone who isn't used to it like me, inadvertently communicated skepticism. As a result, I felt I wasn't coming off as believable, so I became very concerned with accuracy.

For instance, when they asked me how many times I was hit, I had to clarify: "Well, I was kicked once for sure, and I think the rest were with his fists . . ."

"Yes, you were punched," the detective interrupted. I didn't know how he was so sure of that, but he continued. "How many times?"

"Multiple times," I answered, sounding like a nervous witness on the stand.

"Can you give me a number?"

"Between five and eight times? No more than ten."

Looking back, I have no idea why I was so intent on making sure that I didn't overstate things. It was like I wanted to be fair to my attacker.

It was the least I could do if I was going to get him in trouble.

The detective finished his notes and added, "Oh, and one more thing. Don't cancel those credit cards for a couple days. They're usually where we get the best leads."

I looked at Officer Green, like, *dude*? He avoided my gaze.

Finally the EMTs arrived. I was helped into the back of an ambulance where a paramedic took inventory of my injuries.

"Abrasions on legs, arms, foot, laceration on chin, contusions on neck and face. And you got choked, kicked" — he glanced at me — "punched."

"He kicked me once, I think, and then punched? I'm not really sure, it was hard to tell."

He glanced up at me. "Yeah, punched."

Why does everyone keep saying that?

Then he spoke with less certainty. "And, um, were you . . . did the guy try anything, you know, um . . . ?" He made a face.

"You mean, was I sexually assaulted?"

He nodded, looking embarrassed.

I didn't realize EMTs were so delicate. "No, nothing untoward."

He laughed in relief. "Good, because that's a *whole* 'nother *kit.*"

Despite my judging him just a little bit for not being able to say the word "rape" in a professional capacity, we became buds. He told me I should walk with a dog for protection. I told him I had one, but he could only kill you with cuteness. He said he had two Rhodesian ridgebacks, and I impressed him with my Westminster-nerd knowledge of the breed.

"So can you just clean me up, and I can go home?" I asked.

"You got clocked. Head trauma means you should really go to the hospital."

I was more scared of going to the ER than of having a concussion. In seven years living here, I had carefully and intentionally avoided needing emergency care. I always imagined a New York City emergency room on a Saturday night would be a horror show of gunshot victims, cyclists struck by taxicabs, and mugged joggers.

It occurred to me that, basically, I was afraid of seeing *other* crime victims.

But I knew my mom would kill me if she heard I refused medical treatment, so I took my first ever ambulance ride to the urgent-care center three minutes away.

My cop friends met me at the hospital. I say friends genuinely, because when you're so supremely disconnected as I felt that night, any familiar face is your new best friend. I was happy to see them.

"Hey, what are you guys doing here?"

"If we leave you, technically the call is over, and we could get sent somewhere else. We want to make sure we can drive you home when you're done here."

I was so touched, it was the closest I came to crying all night.

They continued to go above and beyond the call of kindness. Officer Moon let me use his personal phone to call my mom.

When her groggy voice came on the line, I spoke with robotic calm: "Hello, Mom, it's me. First off, I'm fine, and you know that I'm fine, because I'm calling you. Unfortunately, I'm calling you from the hospital, but remember, I'm fine. But I was mugged, not with a weapon, and now I'm here with police and hospital staff and I'm fine. Really."

"I'm getting up and getting in the car," she said.

"What, why? That's crazy, it's too late. Drive up tomorrow."

That I thought for one minute that my mom would stay in bed after this call proves I was definitely concussed.

She later told me I sounded like a lawyer.

Before I settled in my room, I had to use the ladies' room. The bathroom mirror was the first time I got a look at myself.

I was stunned.

My head was misshapen. Swelling had puffed out my entire jawline and one eye. The length of my neck was purple, and the bottom of my chin split. My face was covered in cartoonish welts — fat, red knuckle marks across my forehead, temple, cheek, and mouth.

I should've been horrified, but I was actually pretty impressed with myself. I looked badass.

And no wonder everyone knew I had been punched. Above my eyebrow, there was a fist print so clearly embossed, if the punk had been wearing a class ring, you could've read the year.

Then again, maybe if he'd had a class ring, he wouldn't be beating the crap out of women to steal their purses.

The officers kept me company in my curtained-off "room." Eventually the doctor cleaned up my wounds and bandaged the deep ones. She smeared bacitracin antibiotic ointment all over my face, like a boxing coach smearing Vaseline. She complimented my shoes, which only had a little blood on them.

I thought she was awesome.

But while my cop bros thought my lack of tears was super-chill, the hospital staff thought I was in complete denial. My doctor didn't want to discharge me from the ER for my emotional well-being.

"Don't you have anyone to call?"

I tried to explain that I'm not a weird loner, I just don't have anyone's number memorized except my mom's.

The doctor urged me to sleep there the rest of the night until someone could come pick me up.

The ER wasn't quite as bad as I thought, but it was not exactly conducive to sleep. A sheet of fabric separated me from a chorus of unsettling human groans and mechanical beeps. Also, the entire back of my dress was soaked and gritty from grappling on the wet ground. Even my underwear was wet.

"We can get you into a hospital gown."

Yes, because being naked would really improve this situation.

I told her I appreciated her concern, but "I really want to go home."

"I just worry, that you're going to get home alone and totally freak out," she said.

"I have a dog." I thought of my sweet-faced Pip wiggling his furry body in greeting. "I feel safe in my home."

It felt good to hear myself say it. It was true.

She gave in, and I was released not long after.

On the ride home, Officer Green let me ride shotgun in the patrol car and stuck his partner in the back. They made me laugh on the ride home, teasing each other about their weight. They both lamented the difficulty of finding healthy food when your

145

shift runs all night. We all expressed a hatred of cardio.

Somewhere along the way, I stopped feeling like a crime victim and felt like their kid sister.

It was almost dawn when we pulled up to my apartment building. I started to thank them and say good-bye, but Officer Moon stopped me.

"You said you have a dog, right? Don't you have to walk him?"

I nodded.

"So get him, we'll walk him with you."

I thought my heart might burst.

And that's how two New York City police officers ended up standing outside in the rain with me, waiting for my dog to choose a place to pee, just so that I would feel safe.

Back inside my apartment, alone, I did not freak out. I scooped up the dog, walked gingerly to my bed, and fell fast asleep.

Safe in the knowledge that while the city can be a scary place, the good guys still outnumber the bad.

It's Not About Me

LISA

I just wanted to add a word or two about
Francesca's assault, because I know that
many of you moms must be wondering how
I reacted, or how you would react, if you
were in my position.

Specifically, if you were awakened by a
telephone call at four thirty in the morning,
and it's from your daughter. Her tone is
tense but controlled, and she begins the
conversation by saying:

"Mom, I'm at the hospital, but I'm okay."

So how did I react?

I would say, well enough.

Or maybe, not terribly.

After all, I'm a rookie at my daughter being assaulted.

But I'm not a rookie of being a mother in
an emergency situation, and I didn't burst
into tears, freak out, or fuss. I stayed calm
because truly I felt calm, if tense. I dressed
quickly, let the dogs out to go to the bath-

room, and got in the car to New York City, where I made it in only an hour and a half.

It's usually a two-hour-and-fifteen-minute drive.

But there was no traffic.

Or maybe I drove faster than I ever had in my life.

When Francesca opened the door to her apartment, I got the first full view of how bruised and battered she was, and you can imagine what I felt like, but the fact is, I kept it inside.

I hid my shock at how distorted her face looked.

I hid my outrage that this had happened to her.

I hid my fear that it could have been so much worse, that she could have been killed.

I hid my fury that someone could do this to her.

Instead, I gave her a massive hug and told her I loved her, which is something I do every single time I see her, so this was no different.

The thing I tried to remember was not to make it about me.

Because I know how smart and loving she is, and I could see that she was trying not to worry me.

And I didn't want her to have to worry

148

about worrying me.

If that sounds like a confusing state of being, it is, but I bet every mother understands what I'm talking about. She had been through something I had no experience with, and I said to myself, give her the space to have her own reaction.

We went back and forth about whether she should go back to bed, and we did, but the detectives arrived early the next morning, and I listened to her tell them the details of the assault, hearing them for the first time.

She remained remarkably calm, even with the detectives.

So did I, hiding my horrified reaction.

Because she wasn't a kid anymore, she was my adult daughter and she was handling things beautifully, including her own emotions.

And I realized I just had to follow her lead and do what she wanted to do, whether that was getting her a new phone, or her glasses fixed, or even a replacement lipstick.

Frankly, I didn't know which was the best thing to do. I didn't know if we should run around and do errands or if we should rest, and I suspect the two of us were in a confused state, trying to hold on to each other and muddle through.

149

And, I think, we did.

And to a certain extent, we still are. Candidly, I think you can see from the essay she has written that she is still processing this crime and will do so in the months to come, maybe even years.

Any victim of violent crime probably goes through the same thing.

So I know she is not alone.

And she'll always have me.

I don't know whether I help her, but I don't think I make things worse.

All I want is to be there for her and not to screw up.

Because mothers screw up all the time, myself included.

It's a given that we love our children, but it's not a given that we love them the right way or give them what they need at any point in time.

And I learned that it doesn't get any easier as our children grow into adulthood.

Life can make a rookie of anyone.

And the best we can do is our best.

And I will always do my best, for her.

And I will always be there, for her.

That's what a mother is, isn't it?

And it never ends.

Because love never ends.

MOTHER MARY FLUNKS
TIME MAGAZINE
LISA

You may have read the article in *Time* magazine, entitled "The Five Things Your Kids Will Remember About You." It was predictably sweetness and light, but none of it reminded me of Mother Mary, who was anything but sweetness and light. She was more olive oil and vinegar.

In fact, I considered the five things that *Time* set forth and compared them to Mother Mary, to see how she measured up, magazine-wise.

You can play along, with your mother.

Or if you've read the previous books in this series, you could probably fill in the same blanks with Mother Mary stories.

But no spoilers.

So don't tell anyone about the time Mother Mary refused to use the discount Batman bedsheets because she didn't want a life-size Batman lying on top of her.

Or the time she took to wearing a lab coat

because it gave her an air of authority, plus pockets for her cell phone and back-scratcher.

Or the time she grabbed her doctor's butt to prove that she was ready for cardiac rehab.

Nobody would believe those stories, anyway.

So, to stay on point about the *Time* magazine article, the first thing that your children are alleged to remember about you is "the times you made them feel safe."

Awww.

How sweet.

Except that with Mother Mary, what I remember are the times she made me feel unsafe.

Because those were truly memorable.

And my general safety was a given, if less dramatic.

For example, when Brother Frank and I were little, we used to fight, which drove my mother crazy. I remember, one day, she yelled at us to stop fighting and we ignored her, so that she took off her shoe and threw it at us.

She missed, but that didn't stop her.

Because she had another foot with another shoe.

So she took that shoe off and threw it at

us, but she missed with that one, too.

We stopped fighting.

You're probably thinking that she missed us intentionally, and I'll let you think that, but you didn't know Mother Mary. She loved us in a fiercely Italian-American sort of way, which meant that motherhood and minor personal injury weren't mutually exclusive.

So lighten up, *Time.*

The second thing in the article was that your children will supposedly remember "the times you gave them your undivided attention," and the magazine advised parents to "stop what you're doing to have a tea party" with your kids.

Again, growing up, I had no doubt that I had my mother's attention, but it was never undivided and she wasn't into tea parties.

But she chain-smoked.

Does that count?

Mother Mary was a real mom, busy doing laundry, cooking dinner, and cleaning the house, and though she was always available, she wasn't staring deeply into our blue eyes. But every night, my family, The Flying Scottolines, would sit on the couch and watch TV, giving it our undivided attention.

We all loved TV, so by the property of association, we all loved each other.

Good enough for me.

The third thing was, your kids will remember "the way you interacted with your spouse."

This doesn't apply to The Flying Scottolines, since the statement assumes that the parents interacted.

You can't win them all.

My parents barely talked to each other, but at least they never fought, and nobody was surprised when they divorced. But happily, they both loved us to the marrow, and my brother and I knew that.

What I learned from growing up in a house with an unhappy marriage is that divorce is better.

And so I'm divorced twice.

Which I think is the good news, considering the alternative.

If I can't have a happy marriage, I'll have a happy house.

The fourth factor was, your kids will remember "your words of affirmation and your words of criticism."

I don't know if Italian-American families have things that can be characterized as words of affirmation, except "I love you."

And as a child, I heard that at least ten times a day.

But I also heard, "Don't be so fresh."

So I grew up thinking that I was lovable and fresh, which might be true.

The last thing in the article was that children would remember "family traditions," like vacation spots and/or game nights.

The Scottolines weren't the kind to have "game nights," but every summer, we did go on vacation to the same brick row-house in Atlantic City, New Jersey. All day long, we played on the beach while my parents smoked, and at night we sat on the front porch while assorted relatives dropped by and the adults talked, drank beer, and smoked into the night. When the mosquitoes got too bad, we all trundled inside the house, where the adults played pinochle until my brother and I fell asleep on the couch, to the sound of their gossiping and laughter, breathing in the smoke from their Pall Malls and unfiltered Camels.

We had no oxygen, but a lot of love.

And it wasn't Norman Rockwell.

But it was perfect.

Looking back, I wouldn't change a moment.

Thanks, Mom and Dad.

I love you.

And I'm still fresh.

BARBARIANS AT THE FRONTGATE
LISA

Today I'm reporting from the front gate of suburbia.

As well as the Frontgate.

I wanted to buy a new chair for outside, because I like to read or work in the sun and I have only two chairs.

I know what you're thinking.

One person for two chairs, what's the problem?

There are five problems, and they all happen to be dogs.

Often when I come outside with my book or my laptop, the dogs are already occupying both chairs. If I move them off one chair so I can sit down, the five of them spend all day fighting over the second chair.

Most people would solve this problem by training the dogs to stop fighting.

But these people never heard the expression, You can't teach an old dog new tricks.

I'm the old dog.

I gave up teaching my dogs anything, and I try to avoid most of my problems, in this case by buying a new chair.

In other words, some people buy dog beds, and other people buy dog chaise lounges.

Anyway, the chaise lounges I have are ancient wrought-iron affairs with basic green cushions, and that's what I wanted.

So I picked up one of the three hundred catalogs that come in the mail, which I usually pounce on and thumb through, fantasizing.

The Frontgate catalog is porn for suburban women.

Everything in the catalog is color-coordinated, monogrammed, and effortlessly glamorous, and I am none of the above, except for effortless.

Which is Frontgate for lazy.

Not to pick on Frontgate, because I looked at a bunch of other catalogs, and you can't just buy a simple reclining chaise lounge anymore, because they don't make them.

I'm here to tell you, exterior furniture has lost its mind.

In every catalog, there were pages and pages of exterior furniture, and none of it looked like it belonged outside. There were fancy long couches with matching club chairs, end tables, dining-room and coffee tables, as well as love seats and even a chair-and-a-half.

To fit your butt-and-a-half.

All of it looked nicer than my inside furniture.

There were at least twelve "collections" of exterior furniture, with names like Hamptons, Palm Springs, and Palermo.

Surprisingly, there was no Philly.

Yo.

The photos showed fleets of overstuffed furniture beside pools and gardens, but it would have been more appropriate in a living room or a conservatory.

You have a conservatory, don't you?

It's next to the library, and Colonel Mustard is waiting for you there.

With a wrench.

Every catalog had pages of multicolored-fabric options for the megacushions in an array of different styles, such as tufted, piped, double-piped, or knife-edge.

For the felony-lover in you.

I flipped the page, looking for normal-weight fabric in basic green, then I came across "outdoor rugs."

I blinked and blinked.

This concept was new to me.

Evidently, now we need outdoor rugs to put under our exterior furniture, to "protect against hot and cold patio and deck surfaces for luxurious underfoot comfort."

I thought that's why we had "shoes."

Not only that, but there were massive gas grills, stainless-steel refrigerators, and tall patio heaters. There was even a TV with a giant projection screen that you can watch outside. And finally, there were curtains, so-called "outdoor draperies," and their purpose was to "help you define the ultimate outdoor room."

What's an outdoor room?

I thought rooms were supposed to be *inside.*

And the whole point of going outside was to *not* be in a room anymore.

Hence the technical term — out.

Isn't this inside-out?

Or upside-down?

I felt dizzy from the possibilities.

If I get an outdoor rug, do I have to vacuum it?

Or do I need an outdoor vacuum?

Do I want to food-shop for an outside refrigerator, too?

Where will I lose the remote for the outside TV?

Hint: check the azalea.

And what's next, moving the bathroom outside?

Oh wait. We used to have outside bathrooms, but we brought them inside.

Back when we were sane.

Bottom line, is it really a good idea to construct a second house in the backyard of the first one?

The thought makes me tired.

I'm going outside to lie down.

On the grass.

The ultimate outdoor carpet.

MILESTONE OR MILLSTONE?
LISA

By the time you read this, I will have turned sixty, and my birthday will have passed.

Hopefully, I won't have passed, too.

I can't say I'm delighted about this birthday. It's not that I hate aging, it's that I hate dying.

This feeling caught me by surprise. Generally, I love my birthday because it always involves chocolate cake.

But now I'm wondering if the cake is compensation for my death, in which case, we need to do better.

Oddly, I didn't realize I was having negative feelings until I got the idea to renovate my kitchen.

Let me explain.

You may remember that a few years ago I planted a perennial garden, which has somehow survived all the beginner mistakes I made. For example, first I watered it too little, then I watered it too much, so much

A much prettier view than stainless steel

in fact that I broke an underground water pipe.

Backhoes were called. It adds a whole new dimension to gardening when you bring in the heavy equipment.

Not to mention expense. I don't want to think about how much that garden cost. After I soaked the flowers, they soaked me.

But the thing is that the garden is now going gangbusters, though most of it is weeds, but that is neither here nor there.

The point is, I like to look at the garden, but there's no window that looks out onto the garden from my kitchen. The only windows that overlook the garden are on either side of the oven. I want to look at flowers, but I'm looking at stainless steel.

So lately I found myself wishing that I could replace the oven with a window or maybe even a door, then I could not only see the garden all the time, but go out into it. And maybe if I put a little flagstone patio there, I could have a cup of coffee and maybe write outside, in my garden.

Plus the garden colors are so gorgeous, with pink primrose, yellow coreopsis, and purple delphinium. And stainless steel is, well, gray.

Like my roots.

I investigated the cost of renovating the kitchen, and while it wasn't massive, it was a chunk of change that left me wondering, can you spend that money on a kitchen, when you're turning sixty?

Shouldn't I be saving it for retirement?

Or at the very least, a walker?

Do people my age renovate their houses? Will we live long enough to see the renovation? Are we still even buying green bananas anymore?

And I'm just one person, so shouldn't I be thinking about downsizing rather than upsizing?

Unfortunately, the only way my sizes ever

seem to go is up.

Not only that, but I started to wonder if I should just be happy with what I have. I already love my house. I've painted it red, orange, yellow, green, and blue. You see I have a thing for color. It's like living in a paintball war.

Plus I just added a sunroom that I love and use as an office. I renovated the sunroom in my fifties, but is sixty the cut-off?

It made me think of the larger question, which is, if renovation is growing, do we ever stop growing? Does the garden? Or the weeds?

Evidently not.

Writing a book is the same way. You can always edit it to make it more like what you want it to be, or what you have in mind, its best version of itself.

So you see where this is going, and now I do, too.

If a book and a garden can always be improved, then so can the kitchen.

And so can I.

No matter how old I am, I'm going to keep trying to grow and improve, into some final edited version of myself, full of color and fun, until I have to type The End.

I want to be a page-turner of a person.

Or a garden so great that you can ignore

the weeds.

And then I can die.

So I just decided I'm giving myself a kitchen renovation as a gift for my sixtieth birthday.

I want to be closer to my daisies.

Until I'm pushing them up.

TOPPING THE LEADER BOARD
LISA

Mama's got a brand-new bag.

As in golf.

Fore!

Watch out, friends!

Stay off the course. Also any adjoining roads in the tri-state area.

When did this insanity start?

After my last birthday when I realized that procrastination is a luxury I no longer have.

And for the past few years, I noticed that when a golf tournament came on TV, I left it on. Not that I actually sat and watched it, but I had it on while I worked, like suburban background noise.

And every time I looked at the TV, the screen showed pretty green grass. The only way to improve it would be to add perennials.

I wonder how many golfers are also gardeners.

Or as I prefer to call us, weeders.

Maybe people golf to escape weeding?

My plan, exactly.

Plus I liked golf on TV because of the whispering voices of the commentators and the polite clapping of the spectators, punctuated by the occasional thwack of the ball.

It all seemed so relaxing, for an alleged sport.

There was no running around, or even exertion in general.

I work up more of a sweat at the mall.

Where I *walk* from store to store.

Shopping is cardio for women.

Just kidding.

I know that women play golf, but I can never find a women's golf tournament on TV.

There's a surprise.

Plus, the golf on TV shows lots of good-looking men.

Hey, I'm not dead.

And all the men in golf tournaments are dressed so nice.

How often does that happen in real life?

Not at the mall, am I right, ladies?

Women dress up for the mall.

God knows why.

We go to the mall because we have nothing to wear, but we have to find something to wear to the mall.

Ironic.

Anyway, to stay on point, men don't bother to dress up for the mall. They just find a chair and flop. If they're dressed up, they must have a funeral after.

Or a wedding.

Or a golf tournament.

Anyway I mentioned my interest in golf to my best friend Laura, and lo and behold, for my birthday, she surprised me with a set of golf clubs!

Wow!

They were women's clubs, a pretty blue with little rhinestones on the bottom, which actually appealed to me.

Diamonds are a golfer's best friend!

And the tag on the golf bag said these clubs had "increased distance, accuracy, and ultimate forgiveness."

Who doesn't need ultimate forgiveness?

These are golf clubs for people with feelings!

Girls!

Also, the clubs have socks that match.

So they're better dressed than I am.

I unwrapped the clubs like the rookie I am, introducing myself to the mysteries of my new hobby.

For example, all golf clubs have numbers. Who knew?

Unfortunately, there was no number 1, 2, 3, or 4 club in my new bag.

My set might be defective.

And one club had an S on it.

For Scottoline!

Another club had a special sock that read DIVINE.

So clearly, somebody has an attitude problem.

Obviously there's a lot I don't know about golf, so I bought a few golf books, then I went online and emailed a bunch of local public and private courses for lessons.

A few of the private places said I had to be sponsored by people to join a club, but I don't know any sponsors, or how much it costs for a membership, or which club has the best-dressed men.

Heh-heh.

But one club said I didn't have to know anybody to take lessons, so I signed up and I'm in!

I have to fit them in on a weekly basis, with my busy schedule of weeding, bicycling, and riding Buddy The Pony. Oh yes, and writing three books a year.

This must be why people retire.

Because earning a living gets in the way of living.

So my life at sixty will be divided into fore

and after.

I start my golf lessons after I come back from tour for our book, *Does This Beach Make Me Look Fat?*

I may even have a title for the next one.

DOES THIS GOLF COURSE MAKE ME LOOK FAT?

UPGRADING THE
MACARONI NECKLACE
FRANCESCA

When it comes to giving a gift to your mother, kids get a pass for a long time. But when your mother has a milestone birthday like sixty, a macaroni necklace will not do.

It was time for me to get my mother a grown-up gift.

This is not to say that I haven't gotten her nice things in the past, but this year I wanted it to be really special. Maybe because I know that my mom is single, I wanted to get her a gift as nice as a husband would get.

Not one of her husbands — a really good husband.

I got in my head that it had to be jewelry.

I'd never bought a piece of fine jewelry before. First, I studied. For months leading up to her birthday, every moment of procrastination was spent searching the websites of jewelers and department stores for every item within my budget.

171

Happy Birthday, Mom!

Since I couldn't afford ninety percent of their inventory, this took less time than you might think.

After obsessively zeroing in on a few favorite options, I decided to make a trip to Cartier. Embarrassingly, I'd dressed up for the occasion. I wore a shirtdress that I thought said, "I use 'summer' as a verb."

Then I took the subway there, because real rich people are cheap.

I arrived at the flagship store on Fifth Avenue. The storefront's heavy, rotating door expelled the dirty city air from entering its pristine interior with a satisfied sigh.

Luxury, vacuum-sealed.

As soon as my feet sank into the cream-colored carpet, I felt self-conscious. Maybe it was just the tiny spotlights dotting the ceiling. I suppose they're meant to make the diamonds sparkle, but it felt like high-end interrogation lights.

Also, there were almost no other customers in the store, so I felt the hopeful eye beams of every sales associate appraising me and their possible commission from behind the glass countertops.

I couldn't make the first move. Thankfully a saleswoman with perfectly lined red lips stepped forward.

She asked if I'd like anything to drink, because the world of Cartier eliminates minor suffering like thirst. "Water, coffee, champagne?"

I said water and immediately regretted it. I should've gone for the booze.

Always go for the booze.

But I didn't feel like I was going to spend enough to earn it. I was surprised they offered me anything. Free liquor? How gracious and generous of them!

I didn't connect that, considering my intended purchase, I had just refused the most expensive glass of free champagne in the world.

Then she asked me if I had a budget in mind. I told her my budget, my voice apologetic.

You know you're a people-pleaser when you feel guilty for giving someone your business.

A true professional, she didn't blink and pleasantly showed me around.

I had three items in contention, which I had reviewed so many times on the website, I could've recited the model number.

But I wanted to seem cool and casual, like I impulse-buy jewelry all the time. So I played dumb and let her explain each piece to me.

"Piece" is how you refer to jewelry if you have a lot of it.

Also, I love spiels. If I'm going to spend this much on a gift, the least they can give me is a good story to tell.

She talked to me about the materials used, the origin of the design, and all available variations. The one detail they don't include is price, unless you ask.

I couldn't afford to be cool. I asked.

It's good I went into the store with a clear and firm budget in my mind, because the consumerist thrill is a real thing. There's a magpie effect when you're looking at those shiny objects; you get hypnotized. Plus the saleswoman got me chatting about my mom and our relationship, which got me thinking about love instead of money.

Can you put a price on Mom?

My bank account can.

I settled on a necklace.

"I'll take it."

The saleswoman beckoned me to a private booth where I sat across a desk from her. I was offered water and candies on a silver tray. I held out my credit card, which she quickly put out of sight somewhere under the desk, so I couldn't suffer the obscenity of seeing her swipe it. We chatted, and she printed out the receipt, an eight-by-ten piece of paper for me to sign with a fountain pen.

My undergraduate thesis wasn't printed on such fine stock.

Again, at no point does anyone say the price aloud. It's too crass.

Then, a new sales associate appeared at my side to present a freshly boxed version of the necklace for my inspection. The item looked perfect, but the box had a small ding in the corner. I touched the dent lightly and frowned.

"We'll find you a new box," the saleswoman said, shooting her colleague a pointed look. He swept away.

I smiled politely, now fluent in their nonverbal language of luxury. She nodded in apology.

They had created a monster.

After I'd approved the new box, we went through the inspection process again after it had been elaborately wrapped in white origami paper and sealed with an actual red-wax stamp. I was impressed. Finally, my gift was placed in its little red bag. I reached for it.

"One more thing." She pulled out a white cardboard bag and put the red bag inside it. The white bag even had a flap over the top to hide it entirely from view.

"Is that a decoy bag so I don't get robbed on the way home?" I joked. Well, half-joked.

She looked at me aghast. Crime, like tap water and curling receipts, do not exist in the world of Cartier. "Oh no, the forecast said it may rain today. This is to protect your bag."

A bag to protect my bag. Of course! I can't present my gift in some rumpled bag. They think of everything.

When I left, the streets looked dirtier than I remembered. Descending to the deepest depths of the M train, I clutched my bag-in-a-bag to my chest like it contained the Hope diamond.

But inside, I was giddy with excitement. You would have thought I had bought my mom a house, I was so happy.

Spending money is so fun!

But of course it wasn't that. It was the feeling of accomplishment when you have achieved a degree of independence and success that allows you to give back to the person who got you there. To indulge the person who sacrificed for you. To repay a debt, or start to.

It was the joy of showing someone that you can take care of them.

I've never been so excited about a present in my life.

When I gave it to my mom, she cried.

And the next day she looked up the price and yelled at me.

THE AMAZING DISAPPEARING MIDDLE-AGED WOMAN

LISA

My garden isn't growing that well, but my garden room is getting bigger by the minute.

You may remember that I have been thinking about renovating the kitchen so that I could see the garden. Presently, when I sit and eat at the kitchen island, I'm facing the aluminum backsplash to my oven, which takes up the entire wall and at its cleanest, hosts my own blurry reflection.

No woman wants to eat watching herself eat.

Especially when the blurriness adds two inches all around, so that it's either the best way to stay on a diet or the fastest route to clinical depression.

There are two windows on that wall of the kitchen, but they flank the oven and are too far apart to see from the kitchen island, so I have been thinking about just replacing the whole wall with French doors and adding a patio, so I could not only see the garden, but step into it.

Cool, right?

And since it was a tricky job, I hired an architect who drew up some plans, and a contractor to price it, which was when I got sticker shock.

It would not be cheap.

Again I revisited the question of whether I deserved it, but the more I thought about it, I thought, not only did I deserve it, but I deserved better.

Or more accurately, I realized the project was going to cost a lot, and if it was going to cost *that much,* then maybe I should put a roof over the patio and get more use out of the room.

Oddly, it seemed the most practical to spend more money.

This would be the same rationale that makes me buy bigger quantities of things on sale, sometimes even things I don't want.

Because it was practical!

But this time it wasn't something that I didn't want. It was something that I wanted after I started thinking about it. And then I couldn't get it out of my head.

Please tell me that I'm not alone in this.

It's like when you paint the living room, then the dining room looks crappy, so you have to paint that, too.

Which is something that I've also done.

By myself, I might add.

I once painted the interior of my entire house on a Memorial Day Weekend.

Yes, it was a small house.

And a very memorable Memorial Day.

Anyway, you see where this is going, with respect to the garden room.

I knew it would mean that I had to draw up new plans and get a new price from the contractor, but if I was going to do it, I wanted to do it right.

Plus I had resigned myself to the new higher costs. Financially speaking, I was over the dog, so I could get over the tail.

So I called up the architect, and he sent a junior architect from his office, and we discussed my new wish to build an enclosed porch. I told him exactly what I wanted it to look like, and he agreed, then went back to the office to draw up new plans.

Happy ending, right?

Not yet.

A month later, they sent me the plans, not for the garden room that we had agreed to, but a little "alcove," which didn't have any French doors or other things that I had wanted and we had agreed to.

I didn't understand.

And I felt a little nervous about it. And

angry. I couldn't process what had happened, and I knew that these drawings were going to cost me a fortune.

I confess that I didn't know what to do, at first.

I had a talk with myself and decided that I had to assert myself, so I called the architect and we had a big conference call and I asked him what had happened. And he said very politely that he had decided that the garden room I wanted wouldn't look very good on my house, so he had simply decided that I should have an alcove instead, which is what the drawing showed.

My mouth went dry.

My heart beat harder.

I tell you these biological details because I want you to understand that I'm not always the tough girl you may think I am, or even that I should be. I felt intimidated and strange, but I didn't say any of that on the phone. I merely said that I wished he had solved the problem differently, either by calling or emailing me before he had these drawings made up, and he apologized.

That was nice, but I told him I wanted to think about what happened.

We hung up, and the more I thought about it in the ensuing days, I got madder and madder.

At myself.

I felt wimpy.

I felt as if a man would have handled the phone conversation differently than I had, maybe even yelled or made a point more forcefully.

I never yell, except at the dogs, and they don't listen.

And even though the architect apologized, I knew that in the end, it would still cost me money.

I wondered if the architect would have even done that to me, if I had been a man.

I wondered if this was sexism, or just merely individual ways of conducting business, but by the third day of rumination, I decided it didn't matter.

I called another architect, and he came to the house yesterday.

I told him about the garden room, and he told me he thought it would look wonderful.

I asked him if he would have done what the first architect had done.

He answered, "No, you just weren't listened to."

And I thought, *Bingo.*

I had forgotten what it feels like to be ignored, ever since my divorces.

No one's around to ignore me anymore.

And I love it. ☺

I feel better and even optimistic, going forward with my new garden room. I lost money with the first architect, but it was a lesson worth paying for.

Sometimes you have to fight for your happy ending.

BACHELORETTE BOUNCER
FRANCESCA

As a bridesmaid at a bachelorette party, you are part-dance-partner and part-security-guard to the bride-to-be. You want the bachelorette to have a VIP experience, and you are the velvet rope. But in order to do that, you have to master the art of bar sign language.

Last weekend, ten friends and I celebrated my BFF's bachelorette at a beachside bar. On the dance floor, we formed a protective circle around the bride-to-be, ready to wrangle, distract, and if need be, repel incoming males.

It didn't take long. That plastic tiara and sash is like the Bat Signal for single dudes.

A man came up behind one of our friends and put his hands on her hips. No words, no introduction, just a butt grab.

Classic creeper move.

She swiveled out of his reach to give him a hint, but he simply stepped forward and replaced his hands. Then she turned to face him and shook her head. He pouted — does that work on any woman that's not a guy's mother? — and attempted to draw her in again.

She held up her left hand and pointed to her wedding ring.

The caveman gave a nod and walked away. As if the faraway husband's proprietary claim was more compelling than the live woman's refusal.

It's the bro-code of troglodytes.

Trog-code.

We need a similarly effective gesture for unmarried girls. Maybe I could just point to my bare ring finger, and that could be the accepted sign for "my fake husband says I'm not into you."

Then there was a weird couple who kept "bumping into" us. The man was dancing with and kissing his girlfriend, and yet he simultaneously tried to grind up on each of us.

If that was their sign language, we didn't get it — and we didn't want to.

Now listen, you have to work hard to offend an attendee of a bachelorette party; we're a generous bunch, especially a single one like me.

I was a gazelle faking a limp.

But I drew the line at truly offensive behavior. What's an example of that? Oh say, when a drunk guy sneaked up behind me and started making out with my shoulder.

"Heh-eyyy," I said, gently pushing him back by his forehead.

He took this greeting as an invitation to throw his arms around me.

"Give me some space," I said, but the music drowned out my words. So I made karate-chop hands showing a gap between them.

Middle-school dance chaperones got some things right.

He flashed his palms and nodded in what I thought was agreement.

But when I turned my back, he went full-starfish on me — suctioned to my back and seemingly with five arms.

I spun around and acted out each word of, "Stop" (traffic cop), "touching" (bear-claw hands), "me" (double-thumbed point at self).

He feigned confusion and came at me with Frankenstein arms.

I found myself playing charades on the dance floor. "YOU ARE BEING TOO GRABBY. YOU'RE GRABBY."

Anyone looking would have wondered

why I was doing an angry version of the chicken dance in this guy's face.

But he got my message: "GO AWAY."

(The shove to the chest helped.)

Finally, a guy made a polite approach with a smile and an extended hand, the universal sign for "shall we dance?"

And dance we did. For an average bar, this guy was Fred Astaire, but built like an NFL wide receiver.

I was twirled, whirled, and dipped.

How many of us have endured a clumsy dip? At best, I'm usually doing a deep backbend, supporting myself by my back leg, just trying not to break my neck.

This was a proper dip: unexpected, secure, and a total thrill.

After that, I was the grabby one.

But the final skill of the bachelorette crew is to know when to call it a night. I said good night to my new friend, and I helped round up our giggly, wobbly girlfriends for a final headcount.

As we piled back into our party bus, a friend asked me about the guy, "You gave him your *real* number? Girl."

A man who can move like that?

I might even let him graduate to words.

TAN, DON'T BURN
LISA

I'm trying to understand when suntan lotion got weird.

I remember the days when baby oil and vinegar counted as suntan lotion.

Yes, you read that correctly.

The Flying Scottolines used to go to the Jersey Shore for two weeks every summer, and Mother Mary would mix baby oil and red wine vinegar in a bottle before we left for a day at the beach.

I have no idea where she got the recipe.

Maybe the Mayo Clinic.

Or the Mayonnaise Clinic.

Anyway, we would slather on baby oil and vinegar, dressing ourselves like a salad. I even used to put lemon juice in my hair, so I was certifiably edible.

Of course, with only condiments for protection against the sun, we turned bright red.

And we thought we looked great.

Like Beggin' Strips, with feet.

I don't think it ever occurred to us to use store-bought lotion. We were like Amish, but Italian.

We passed up Coppertone, which came in only one SPF, -5.

And we would never spring for Bain de Soleil, which squirted like orange toothpaste from a tube. It was the fancy suntan lotion, for rich and/or French people.

Not for Bain de Brigantine.

The only problem was, as good as our sunburns looked, they hurt like hell.

We would hurry to the drugstore for jars of Noxzema, which only made us hurt more, though we smelled less fattening.

After the pain subsided, we started peeling, which we thought was totally fun.

How?

Telling you would be oversharing, but why stop now.

By the way, if you're eating breakfast as you read this, please stop. That is, stop eating. You should never stop reading, especially if you're reading anything I write.

Anyway the overshare is that my father's back used to peel the worst of all of us, and so at night, Brother Frank and I would have a lot of fun peeling the skin off his back for him.

Ewwww.

Okay, in our defense, this was before the Internet.

There weren't a lot of things to do, back then.

TV only had three channels, and for us, peeling each other's backs counted as entertainment.

Sometimes my dad's skin peeled off like eraser rubbings, but other times, it came off like potato chips.

Score!

I'm not trying to gross you out, I'm telling you this because I was reminded of the eraser rubbings last week, when I started to use one of these newfangled suntan lotions, all with an SPF higher than balsamic.

One was a lotion that claimed to be "lightweight," so I slathered that everywhere.

Because I want to be lightweight.

Especially if all I have to do is put on lotion.

But ten minutes later, I happened to touch my arm, and I noticed that there were eraser rubbings everywhere I had put the lotion.

Which made no sense.

I'd used the lotion so my skin wouldn't peel, but the lotion was peeling.

And without any of the bright red fun.

So I washed it off. Then I tried another kind of suntan lotion, which I sprayed on. By the way, I don't know when spray cans started being okay. Maybe it's kosher to destroy the ozone layer to keep it from destroying you.

This second type was a "sport" suntan lotion, and my idea of a great sport is spraying myself with suntan lotion.

The can allegedly had "AccuSpray," but when I aimed it on my back, the lotion fogged everywhere, coated my hair, and glued my ponytail to my neck, which is always a good look for a single girl.

So I washed that off, too.

I ended up with the third kind of lotion, called Water Babies.

It was "Pediatrician-Recommended," so I think it was perfect for me.

The SPF matched my age.

Bain de Senior Citizen.

Protect the Candle
LISA

I just hung up the phone, having said no to going out to lunch.

And about an hour ago, I said no to a speaking engagement that would've been wonderful.

And yesterday, I said no to somebody who wanted to invite me to drinks and dinner at a local golf club.

Do you think I'm being negative?

On the contrary.

I'm being positive.

Because I've come to realize that my time really is precious.

Not only in monetary terms, but more in its scarcity.

And I've come to realize that every time I say no to someone else, I am saying yes to myself.

What am I talking about?

Let me explain, because if I have any accumulated wisdom in all these decades,

192

it is this:

You need to protect the candle.

What does that mean?

Here's where I got the image, and it's not overly impressive. It's not from great literature, but from old-fashioned scary movies.

Remember those movies, where the family is in the dark mansion at night and they hear a noise, and it's in Victorian times, so there's no electricity. In the next scene, a beautiful woman with a long braid and wearing a cotton nightgown will invariably grab a candle, light it, and walk around the house in the dark, cupping her slim, elegant hand in front of the candle's flame.

Think Nicole Kidman during a power outage.

She cups the candle for obvious reasons, so the candle won't blow out, since it's a fragile thing and could be extinguished by the slightest breeze, not to mention some terrifying ghost.

And for some reason, as my writing career progressed, I began to feel the squeeze of lots of obligations and requests, barking like dogs in the yard.

I'm not complaining, because I know how lucky I am, but truth is I think my life is exactly like yours in this respect.

You might have a job that you need to do,

or you have a child you want to devote time to, or an elderly parent that needs your attention. Or you simply want to set fifteen minutes aside every day to do yoga, start your own book, or cook an incredibly complicated French recipe.

In the lives of modern women, there is a constant tension between the things we want to do and the things we ought to do, and it's impossible to balance these things.

Especially when, at least in my case, I've spent a lifetime confusing the things I want to do with what other people want me to do.

I'm a people-pleaser, from birth.

But as time wore on, and my nerves got more frayed than they needed to be, I thought as many people as I pleased, I really never got to please myself.

To do whatever I wanted to do.

Even if what I wanted to do was clear my head and write my book, which is my actual job.

People who don't work at home don't get that home is work.

And finally, after decades of this madness, I came to the realization:

I have to protect my candle.

My candle was the stories I wanted to tell, in my books.

And what I started to do was to say no to anything that wasn't those things.

My image at all times was the woman in the nightgown with the long braid, cupping her hand in front of her flickering candle.

And even though it sounds simple to say no, it wasn't, not for me.

People asked repeatedly, which I came to realize was pressure.

Others became angry at me when I said no.

I lost a few acquaintances, and one or two friends.

I missed out on some boring parties, and some great ones.

But the more I protected my candle, so that I spent my energy and time on what I loved, the happier and happier I got.

You may be more enlightened than I, in which case you might be rolling your eyes by now.

But if you're like me, I hope you take my advice, because it is the only thing I know for sure:

Protect your candle.

And what is your candle?

Whatever you want to do.

Trying tai chi.

Reading a novel.

Writing a novel.

Learning Spanish.

Watching *Real Housewives.*

Sunbathing.

Whatever you want, it's completely up to you.

Something you love.

And then, make that the thing you say yes to, every time.

If you have to do a job that isn't your candle, give time to your candle every day.

Protect that time like a maniac.

Put your hand in front of the flame and don't let anybody blow your candle out.

Give yourself the permission to say no to the requests of others.

To disappoint them.

To even make them angry.

If they get mad at you because you did something else that you wanted to do more, you don't need them in your life.

And the interesting thing is that the more things you say no to, you feel that you are paring your life down, but you'll be expanding it, because the time you give yourself allows you to grow in new directions, which arise organically from something you truly love to do.

And in time, you may come to the same realization that I did recently.

Which is that the candle isn't a project at all.

The candle is you.

Unhappy Madison
LISA

It has come to this:

I love golf.

The only problem is, golf doesn't love me.

So I picked up the phone, called a bunch of golf courses, and finally found an instructor who would take me as a beginner.

He had no idea how much of a beginner I was.

Until I showed up the first day, and he had to unwrap the cellophane off the putter, which I had missed.

And since then, I've made every mistake in the book.

My first lesson set the tone, because when I was getting ready at home that morning, I had the first question every woman has:

What to wear?

I had been working and hadn't had a chance to go buy golf clothes, but I figured, how different could golf clothes be from normal clothes?

Answer: Different.

For example, it was a sweltering ninety degrees outside, so I put on a nice pink tank top, gray gym shorts, and running sneakers.

Wrong, wrong, wrong.

I drove to the golf club and parked at the appointed place, which turned out to be the driving range. I got out of the car, grabbed my bag of clubs, and hoisted them over my shoulder, then surveyed the crowd lined up at the driving tees.

I was the only woman.

I was also the only tank top.

Gym shorts.

And running shoes.

My instructor turned out to be a handsome young golf pro named John, who flashed me a friendly smile, introduced himself, and shook my hand.

To which I replied, "Am I dressed funny, or is it just that I have ovaries?"

He wasn't sure whether or not to laugh, because he wasn't used to me yet. He answered, "You might want to get a pair of golf sneakers."

"Okay, will do."

"Also, please don't take this the wrong way, but your shorts are too short."

I felt my face flush. It had been a long time since I felt like a whore in public.

199

Maybe since hot pants.

Please tell me you remember hot pants.

You don't? Well, they looked like a satiny version of my gym shorts, which I don't think were that short, reaching the middle of my thigh. Showing off my upper thigh isn't on the agenda, unless one of your favorite foods is cottage cheese.

"Really?" I asked him, dry-mouthed with embarrassment. "These are normal gym shorts."

"Yes, but golf shorts should go to your knee."

"Oy," I said.

Which is a lot more polite than, "Are you freaking kidding me?"

John cleared his throat. "Also, if you're going to wear a sleeveless shirt, it has to have a collar. If it doesn't have a collar, it has to have sleeves."

"So a tank top is a no-go?"

"Correct."

"Can I stay even though I'm dressed wrong?"

"Of course. You didn't know. Just next time, it would be great if you dressed ap-propriately." John gestured to my golf bag. "I can carry that for you."

"That's okay," I said, because I was Making A Point. Just because I'm a woman doesn't mean I can't carry my own bag.

"You sure?" John asked.

"Yes, no worries."

By the way, I always say "no worries" when I really mean the exact opposite.

I wish there were an expression for women like me, which would probably be, "Worries."

Anyway, John took off across the beautiful green grass, and I quickened my pace to keep up.

John said over his shoulder, "Please don't run, it tears up the grass."

"Oh, oops!"

So I felt not only like a whore, but I felt like a stupid whore.

"Also," John said gently, "lower your voice."

"Sorry."

Well, you get the idea.

I was a golf virgin, but somehow I ended up feeling like a stupid, *loud* whore.

But that was then and this is now.

John turned out to be the nicest guy in the world, in addition to being a superb instructor. I am loving golf, even though I've had only five lessons.

Which is four more than you need to

figure out that golf is an impossibly difficult game.

Even for a well-dressed woman, like me.

BREAKING AND RENTER-ING
FRANCESCA

I always feel like a creeper in a rental house. Unlike the pristine blankness of a hotel room, a rental house is covered in proof of someone else's ownership. Just walking around the rooms feels like snooping. You're sleeping in someone else's bedsheets, browsing someone else's books, eating someone else's leftovers.

You're like a benevolent burglar.

Which is part of the fun!

As long as the house doesn't fight back.

The week of July Fourth, four friends and I stayed in a house that seemed booby-trapped. The house used everything short of poltergeists to communicate hostility to our being there.

My friend's boss had rented the house and was letting her use it for a week as a work perk. When we first arrived, we saw a note he'd left for us:

"Glass table broke. Service guy coming to

The beautiful deck we couldn't walk on and the inviting pool with broken glass on the bottom

clean this afternoon. Wear shoes on deck."

We looked outside. "Broke" wasn't the right word. The glass table had exploded. A layer of glass shards blanketed the wooden deck like snow.

Sharp, dangerous, foot-slicing snow.

There were even pieces glittering at the bottom of the pool.

We opened the sliding door to get a better look and heard a *beep*.

"What was that?" I asked.

"Oh, it says, 'child-safe alarm.' " My friend peered at a small box by the door. "I guess to alert parents if the kid goes out to the pool alone."

I nodded. "Smart."

Then a siren pierced the air with a wail so loud we ducked for cover.

The beep was the warning; the siren was the alarm.

Mercifully, we closed the door and it silenced. But it took trial and earsplitting error to figure out how the alarm system worked:

If you opened any of the three doors leading to the back, you had ten seconds to exit and close the door again, or the siren would go off. And the kicker?

The doors locked automatically behind you.

An alarm system that forces you to keep an un-air-conditioned house hermetically sealed in July *and* forces you to lock yourself out?

Not smart.

The alarm struck me as more anti lawsuit than anti drowning.

We couldn't live with this all week, so we set about figuring out how to disable it without permanent damage. My friend has a head for engineering, so she performed surgery to the back of it.

It was like the game Operation, with a

more annoying penalty sound.

On Independence Day, two of my friends, including our host, left for a thirty-mile bike ride. Exercising my American right not to exercise on vacation, I stayed back, along with the other two. We had heard of a lawn party nearby and decided to check it out.

We were in the car ready to go when my guy friend realized he forgot something. He jogged back to the house while we waited. A minute later, we heard the burglar alarm go off.

It was a tremendous sound from halfway down the driveway. We ran to the house to help, and at the front door, it was deafening.

Our poor guy friend clutched his ear with one hand while frantically pushing buttons with the other.

If the security system was like the one I grew up with, the next step was a call from the alarm company that we'd have to answer and explain it was a false alarm or the cops would come. I ran into the house to look for the house phone, but we'd been using our cells all week, I had no idea where they kept the actual telephone. God knows I couldn't hear it ring.

By now, the blaring alarm was causing

brain damage. We bailed and ran out of the house.

As soon as we landed on the lawn, the alarm finally stopped.

"I swore I got the code right," my guy friend said.

"What do we do now, will the police come?" asked another. We weren't afraid of arrest, but we didn't want to get our host in trouble with her boss.

I had the idea that we should call the security company and report the false alarm, you know, "get ahead of it."

I saw that on *Scandal.*

I found the little lawn sign from the company and Googled the main number.

Then I waited on hold for twenty-three minutes. In case of an actual home invasion, that response time seemed less than ideal.

Finally, a representative answered; I gave her the address of the house and told her what happened.

"What's the name on the account?" she asked.

"I'm not sure. We're just renters."

"Okay, but who are you renting from?"

"Um . . ." I looked to my friends, but they didn't know either. "We're not sure. Our friend is the main renter, well, technically her boss is, and they're not here right now, so . . ."

"I can also look it up with the home phone number."

I had never found the house phone, and I definitely didn't know the number. "We don't know that either."

It sounded bad. We had zero of the information a plausible renter would know. I began to doubt my wisdom of "getting ahead of it" by essentially reporting our own burglary to a security company in the shadiest way possible.

We were guilty of breaking and renter-ing.

The customer service woman asked me to repeat the address. I bit my lip as I listened to her rapid typing, almost certain she was forwarding it to police dispatch.

"There's no active account for that house. Sometimes people have our security system installed, but then stop paying for our services and leave the alarm."

I thanked her and hung up, relieved.

Another clever alarm by the house's owners. These hair-trigger security systems may or may not succeed in scaring off burglars, but they'll sure as heck scare off repeat renters.

SPAGHETTI AND SALAD
LISA

They say you should never talk about politics or religion.

But these days, politics is religion.

And I think that's a wonderful thing.

This way, instead of not talking about two things separately, you can not talk about two things together.

This is much more efficient.

It's like if you were going to have dinner of spaghetti and salad. In the old days, we ate them separately, but these days, we mix the spaghetti and the salad together and eat them that way.

Doesn't that sound delicious?

Isn't that better?

This way, we're doing two things at once, and we all know that that always yields better results.

Except when you're driving.

The one thing we all agree on is that drinking and driving is not for the betterment of society.

Neither is texting and driving.

Or talking on the phone and driving.

Or doing anything else but driving while you're driving, but nevertheless, people do this every day.

We love to combine things.

That's how we roll.

Usually we're rolling into a divider, but never mind that right now.

It's interesting to contrast today with the way things used to be. Because if you look back, history didn't combine things the way we do.

For example, our forefathers did not see the wisdom in combining things. They were old-fashioned that way, and I'm sure they didn't eat spaghetti and salad together.

They didn't think politics and religion should be combined, and in fact they wrote that down on a piece of paper, like a Things To Do List for America.

One of the items on the list was to Keep Church and State Separate.

But what did they know?

And who does everything on their Things To Do List?

Overachievers.

Obviously, we've improved on that separation-of-church-and-state nonsense this political season, when the first thing every politician tells you is which God he believes in, how much harder he believes in his God than the other politicians, and which God qualifies you to be the best politician.

Good to know.

By the way, just so we're clear, both Democrats and Republicans do this.

Which is all for the better.

It makes politics a lot easier for everyone.

Because then you can just choose the guy who's on the same team you are and that saves the politician the time of thinking up anything good for the country.

(Or you.)

And it also saves the politician the time he'd spend talking about the economy, unemployment, war, education, health care, and other issues that are totally boring.

I myself am going to vote for the most religious politician I can find. He should wave a Bible in each hand and balance one on his head at the same time that he recites from one.

In fact, if he could juggle Bibles, he should be president.

Automatically.

That's my religious test.

Who can juggle the most Bibles?

Anyway, in the midst of these extremely pious politicians comes Pope Francis, a bona fide religious leader.

And he didn't even talk about religion.

True, he talked about God, but he didn't speak only to his team, and he talked to people who don't believe in God at all.

Can you think of a single politician who will say something nice about atheists?

Instead, the Pope talked about the golden rule.

He said we should be closer to one another and support each other.

He talked about how we should take care of the less fortunate among us.

And he showed what he thought we should be doing, by hugging people, kissing babies, and visiting the sick and senior citizens.

Others talked about religion for him, and they set up his stage with all the stuff, symbols, and signs.

And all of the politicians who introduced the Pope talked about religion more than he did.

The politicians pandered to the Pope.

This can't be helped.

They wake up like this.

They tell people what they think people want to hear.

So they can get what they want from

people, which is your vote and your money.

But Pope Francis didn't want anything from anybody.

Except to send a message.

And the message was love.

I'll vote for that.

Holiday FOMO
FRANCESCA

Why are we always so anxious to do something cool on a holiday?

On any average weekend, I have my choice of movie dates, improv shows, and some friend's band concerts to go to. But come Halloween, New Year's, Labor Day, or Cinco de Mayo, I'm always scrounging for plans.

This happened again this Fourth of July. I thought I was safe from holiday FOMO, Fear Of Missing Out, since I was spending the week with pals at that Hamptons rental. But then Independence Day arrived, gray and rainy — two of my friends had taken their bikes out early, while the remaining three of us, myself, a girl, and a guy, found ourselves sitting around the living room, half-reading, half-looking at our phones, experiencing existential crises via Instagram and Facebook.

Codependence day.

Even when I have plans, there's nothing to do.

But then that glorious sound, mechanical and yet angelic:

A text message chimed in on my phone.

It was from this guy I'd been crushing on, and it read: "Are you coming to the lawn party for the Last Chance Animal Rescue? It's EPIC."

Not the typical adjective to describe a daytime charity benefit. I replied, "I'm imagining a DJ while holding a kitten with headphones on."

"That's actually happening."

My friends and I were intrigued. Also desperate. At the very least, this sounded like something we could exaggerate on social media.

We hopped in the rental car, and headed out.

When we put the address into our GPS, the pin dropped in the center of unidentified green space. As we drove along on the winding, wooded road, we began to see cars parked along the street.

"Is this for the party?"

"It can't be, the GPS says we're still five minutes away."

But as we went on, more and more cars were parked, some dangerously close to blind curves, until the road was completely lined with them.

We tucked our rented Toyota Corolla behind a red BMW convertible and walked the rest of the way. As we got closer, we could hear dance music thumping through the forest.

"Seriously, what is this?" my friend asked.

We were about to find out. We followed others to the base of a long driveway, the sides of which were clearly reserved for the prestige cars. Porsches were the most common, but I also saw a couple Bentleys, a Maserati, and lots and lots of these boxy Mercedes SUVs styled to look like military vehicles, presumably marketed to civilian men with small penises.

Another thing that became clear as we hiked up the drive in our flip-flops was that we were not dressed appropriately for this "lawn party." The women exiting these cars were dressed to the nines: hair blown out, false lashes, sky-high heels, designer duds.

The men were dressed more casually, but they wore the women like accessories. A guy with a popped collar passed us flanked on either side by two model-thin women in those Herve Leger bathing suits that you can't get wet, sheer chiffon cover-ups, and gladiator stilettos sandals. All three wore designer sunglasses, and none was smiling.

"No, but *seriously,* where are we?"

We walked over to an information table manned by a model-thin woman and about six burly bouncers.

She greeted us, and said there was a donation to get in.

I didn't see any signage for a charity anywhere. "This benefits the animal rescue?"

"A portion does."

I opened my wallet to see what I could give.

"It's fifty for women, two hundred for men."

I looked at her, aghast.

She smiled. "We accept credit."

First off, charging different prices for men and women is demeaning at a nightclub, but at a charity benefit? And second, three hundred bucks to drink beer outside, and we wouldn't even get to hold a puppy? She had to be out of her mind.

We decided to bail. The whole way back down the drive, we giggled at how bizarre the scene was. The level of privilege was insane, and we said that knowing we were plenty privileged ourselves.

My guy friend shook his head. "I'm just glad we parked the Corolla down the street."

But we were also poking fun at it to re-assure each other that we weren't missing out on the most glamorous, *epic* Pimp-My-Animal-Shelter Party ever.

At the base of the driveway, an unusual scene caught my eye: a couple that had just exited a cab.

"You are so adorable, you have to take a picture with me!" the woman squealed.

The driver, an older Indian man, looked uncomfortable as the woman made a series of hot-girl poses beside him and her boy-friend snapped pics on an iPhone.

I wasn't sure what I was watching, but it gave me a bad feeling in my stomach.

"Ohmigod, thank you, you're so cute," she said and scampered away. The driver got back in the car, and the couple walked up the driveway toward us.

As they passed, I overheard the girl snicker. "He smelled *so* bad."

It sucked the glamour out of the scene for sure.

We spent the rest of the afternoon explor-ing the town, getting fancy with our recipe plans for our July Fourth feast, buying fish and clams right off the dock. The three of us got a head start on the cooking before our amazing cyclist pals got home, and we all finished dinner in time to get a primo

No FOMO here

fireworks-watching spot on the beach.

While we were lying on our backs in the sand, we tried to describe the party to our other friends, but they didn't believe us. So, I Googled it, and I found an article with the following details:

The property where the party was held was the home of TV *Hercules* Kevin Sorbo, rapper Ja Rule was there, a small fire got started, two people nearly died from alcohol poisoning, and the cops shut it down less than an hour after we left.

If we didn't know better, we would've been afraid we'd missed a great party.

GAME OF THRONES
LISA

If you read me, you know that I get jazzed about certain products.

And then I spread the word, herein.

I'd like to do that right now, with a short preface before I get to the point.

This, instead of my usual endless preface before I get to the point.

Getting to the point isn't all it's cracked up to be.

So here we go.

First, my favorite product in the world is my books.

And thank you for your support.

Second, any one of my books would go very nicely with the product I am about to recommend, but this is where we come to another preface. The following is for mature audiences only.

Also my readers.

If you like what I write about, and the way I write about it, you should feel free to keep reading. I say this with confidence because if you meet all of the above criteria, then you have endured stories about bunions, gray chin hairs, and adult diaper rash. And through my misadventures, I've recommended products I love, like Boudreaux's Butt Paste, ThermaCare, and Bradley Cooper.

In other words, you know way too much about me and you don't mind. Maybe you can relate.

Or you have a strong stomach.

And a great sense of humor.

Even if your breasts sag.

So what?

Unsaggy breasts aren't all they're cracked up to be, either.

I mean, we get it, girls.

Soon you'll be us.

Anyway, to inch closer to my point, there's an ick factor to the discussion of my second-favorite product, so if I haven't cured you of your prissiness so far, check out now.

Because we're entering the throne room with my favorite new throne.

The Squatty Potty.

I don't know if you've heard about it, but it's my new love.

I heard about the Squatty Potty on the radio, and I thought it sounded like an interesting idea. Bottom line, and no pun, it's basically a stool that fits around the base of your toilet, and so when you sit on the toilet, it raises your legs into a squatting position.

Still with me?

Good. Either way. You can't please everybody, and the people who continue to read will have their life changed.

Or at least their colon.

By the way, I have no problem in the bathroom.

Only in the bedroom.

In that I sleep with five dogs and a remote control.

Plus I'm no doctor, but I believe the Squatty Potty website, which says that squatting relaxes the puborectalis muscle, or basically, a kink in your colon. When you use your Squatty Potty, your colon gets un-kinked.

Again, not a medical term.

I have a J.D., not an M.D.

But I like the idea that a squatting position is more natural for your anatomy. It may be a sign of the times that I've fallen in love with a toilet, but I don't view it as being about elimination. I view it as being about my health and by my health I mean me living as long as humanly possible and then some.

I want you to live that long, too, especially if you're buying my books.

I always used to think about death. I truly wonder what will kill me, but unfortunately as soon as I find out, I'll be dead.

Everything has a catch.

But I do find myself being more conscientious about eating healthy foods and exercising even when I don't want to.

Let's pretend golf is exercise.

Everybody else does.

But my favorite exercise of all is sitting down, and now I can sit down and know that I'm getting healthier, every time I'm in the throne room.

Look at it this way.

If you don't want to do squats, you can just, well, squat.

FACETS OF A STONE

FRANCESCA

I think I had a panic attack.

It was the middle of the night, I was lying in bed in a quiet beach house, but I was up, thinking, always thinking when it's dark — when my heart rate suddenly sped up. There was no specific thought that triggered it, no particular emotion I could identify to make sense of it. But I felt like I had been injected with something, a drug, adrenaline. I tried to take a deep breath, but couldn't. My heart was racing now, going so fast it scared me. I sat up and brought my hand to my chest, as if I could catch it by the tail.

The assault had taken place two weeks prior. I had spent the first week at home with my mother recovering from the worst of my physical injuries, then I had accepted my friend's serendipitous offer to share her week in the Hamptons. This was the last night in the beach house before I was supposed to return to New York, fully recovered.

A few days later, our book tour began. Spooked by the panic attack, I'd decided that I wasn't ready to turn the mugging into a story to tell on tour. But I had to briefly address it, because I had posted about it on Facebook when it happened, and because I still had visible injuries on my legs. The response from our readers was uniformly concerned and kind.

And yet on the car ride home after our first signing, I was in tears.

With each person who smiled in relief and said, "You're so lucky," or "Thank goodness it wasn't worse," I felt more and more guilty that I wasn't feeling more happy and healed. With every person who told me I was strong, I felt weak and phony.

Ironically, I had felt both happy and lucky when it had first happened.

The swell of emotion when I saw a group of people running toward me seconds after my assailant had gone might best be described as catastrophic relief. I had thought I could die, I had fought for my life, and I had escaped without grave injury. When help arrived, I was manic with gratitude and excess adrenaline. Even when the exhaustion began to hit, I was sanguine.

I was the one who had spent the following weeks telling everyone how "lucky" I was, putting their fears to rest, reminding them it could've been worse, shit happens.

But the feeling didn't stick.

I was still obsessively reliving the attack every night, going over it second by second, trying to fill in the blank spots where fear or injury had damaged my memory. I felt scared walking alone at night. I cut the last dog walk before bed short, sometimes just walking back and forth up and down my block.

I told the story to anyone who asked — even though recounting it made my heart race — until I ended most social interactions fatigued. I wasn't seeking out attention or sympathy, on the contrary, my friends' and family's concern made me uncomfortable, but it was like I had to purge the experience. I wanted to say it out loud enough times so that it did become a "story," a collection of words in a particular order, divorced from visceral memory. I wanted to transform an attack that rendered me helpless into words that I controlled.

I might still be trying to do that.

But the process drained me. I was receiving many kind messages from friends via email and Facebook, but replying left me mentally and emotionally derailed. Sometimes I let the messages sit in my inbox, starred, and didn't reply at all — which made me feel so guilty.

I still stay up some nights drafting my apologetic responses.

The D.A. assigned to my case encouraged me to avail myself of free counseling provided by the city to crime victims. After the book tour, I waited over an hour in the Office of Victims' Services, an overworked department located in the courthouse downtown. I was given a stack of forms to fill out to qualify for medical compensation, counseling, etc.

Every fourth question began, "In the case of deceased victim . . ."

It reminded me how many people using these services are bereaved, and how many of the victims lost their lives.

And I wanted counseling because someone roughed me up?

I was lucky. It could've been so much worse.

I filled out the forms but didn't follow up.

I didn't need help, or I decided, I shouldn't.

Judging all of my emotions became a common theme. I didn't want to suppress my feelings, but I didn't want to wallow. I wanted to face my fears, but not indulge them. I put enormous pressure on myself to recover the *right* way, the emotionally healthy, mentally strong way.

To do whatever it takes not to let this leave a mark.

"Victim" has never been a label I'm comfortable with, anyway. I was afraid once you took on that role, you could never shake it.

I was most afraid of being afraid.

That I had made a life on my own in New York was one of my proudest accomplishments. I lived alone and I loved it. I considered myself a strong, independent, savvy woman, like all the women I admire most, like my mother. These were the traits I liked most about myself.

And suddenly I felt they were under siege.

My remaining negative feelings after the assault didn't just threaten my sense of safety, they threatened my very identity.

The night that it happened, the police needed to know the house address nearest to the location of the attack, but I struggled to recall exactly where I had been when it started.

"You had an umbrella, right? Look for that," the cop said.

I had completely forgotten. With all my

things taken from me, it was hard to remember what I'd started with. We drove a few hundred feet more, when I saw it.

My pink, floral-print umbrella lay on the ground utterly destroyed. It was inside out and half-smashed, the nylon fabric torn from its metal limbs, the arms bent back unnaturally.

I remember thinking, if that's what happened to my umbrella, what had happened to me?

That anxiety was part of what spurred my actions the day after the attack. I wanted to do everything I could to return things to normal, by force if necessary.

I declared that Sunday my "day of defiant fun." My mom wanted me to rest, cancel plans, but I refused. I convinced her to eat brunch at my favorite restaurant and sit outside, because "brunch must go on!" I had my mom take a picture of this victory brunch to post on Facebook.

It took several tries to get a shot where I looked the least injured.

My mom said all the pictures made her sad and deleted them from her phone.

We walked all over my neighborhood to replace what was stolen, from my iPhone to my favorite lipstick, parading my injured body instead of hiding it. I took my mom to the exact spot where I was attacked. I wanted to see it in the daylight, holding my mom's hand, and dispel the bad juju.

I made her take some gag photos on that spot, too.

Again, I wanted to retake control over that physical space. I lived in this neighborhood, and I didn't want to cede any territory to a bad experience.

But I'd be lying if I said it wasn't influenced by the fact that my mother was behind the camera. I wanted badly to prove to both of us that I was okay.

I was probably pushing myself too much when I insisted we keep our prior plans with friends to go to the Broadway Bares benefit show that night. I was exhausted, my voice was completely gone, but canceling something fun and positive felt like admitting defeat.

When we were getting ready to leave my apartment, I realized my new iPhone hadn't restored my contacts list and needed more time on the Wi-Fi network. I said I wanted to wait. My mom said we had to go, or we would be late.

"We won't be late, it will only take ten minutes," I said.

She insisted that it was rude to keep them waiting.

I exploded. "It's useless without the contacts! What if I get separated from the group? I don't know anyone's number. I just went through this, I can't not have my phone!" I burst into tears, surprising us both.

It was the first time I had cried in front of her, and the first time I had cried since the assault, over a phone.

But I had been white-knuckling it through the lingering sense of vulnerability for the last twelve hours. After feeling stripped bare the night before, I needed the security of a working cell phone.

It was the first crack in my defiantly cheerful façade.

Which is not to say that my behavior that day was artifice. I genuinely wanted to do these things, and I derived real satisfaction from testing and proving my own resilience. But my victory lap belied a fear and anxiety about change — deep down, somewhere I couldn't yet articulate, I was acting defensively.

I didn't want the stain to set.

I didn't want to be "damaged."

There's a pervasive narrative in books, TV, and movies about damaged women. We see many depictions of traumatized women, women with baggage, fragile women in need of protection and special consideration but just as often abandoned for being too complicated. It's portrayed as a status, not a journey.

But as time went on, I found the starkness of that definition wasn't working for me. It didn't fit my lived experience of trauma and its aftermath, which was proving to be paradoxical. I had to allow for the contradictions I was experiencing.

Yes, I am lucky that it wasn't worse, but no, it wasn't my lucky night. I can be grateful for my current health and the people who helped me, while still acknowledging my own suffering. I can get scared and still be strong. Courage doesn't exist without fear.

Resilience, in human beings, doesn't mean snapping back to normal fast as a rubber band. Resilience begins from the first moment of challenge and continues every day after to meet it. Resilience and struggle are often one and the same.

The way reading often delivers you exactly what you need, I happened to come across an Elizabeth Gilbert quote that reflected my revised view. She wrote, "The women whom I love and admire for their strength and grace did not get that way because shit worked out."

Mental fortitude doesn't require you to maintain a pristine existence, and real life doesn't allow for that anyway. Emotions, even riotous ones, are the antibodies to a traumatic experience. I have to let them do their work.

Once I gave myself the permission, the freedom, and the time to feel my emotions without judgment, my anxiety began to subside. I haven't had another panic attack since, but if I do, I won't take it as a blow to my identity. I am still the woman I thought I was, and I am still on my way to becoming the woman I want to be.

Like a diamond has many facets, there are many sides to a strong woman. As I go through the spectrum of life experience, I find more and more angles to catch the light.

This Call Is Being Monitored for Quality Assurance Purposes

LISA

If you've read what Daughter Francesca and I have written about Mother Mary, you can guess how she would react to the following story.

In fact, you have to guess.

Because I can't print her reaction here.

We begin with the fact that Mother Mary passed away, leaving a bank account with some money. It wasn't a lot, which was a fact she used to joke about. She'd say:

"I'm set for life, if I die next week."

God love her.

Sadly, she did pass, and I was named POD on her account, which means payable on death.

This will get funny soon, I hope.

So naturally, I went to the bank to get the money, and they told me I have to produce her death certificate. This, even though they had already been notified of her death and closed the account.

But okay.

I get that.

So I went back to the bank with her death certificate, and they told me I had to fill out a "Letter of Instruction," get it notarized, and mail it to the address they provided.

By the way, the instruction in the letter is to mail me a check because I am POD, even though that is exactly what POD means.

But okay, I get that, too. We have rules and regulations, and this is America.

The bank told me that I would receive a check in ten days.

Three months later, I still hadn't gotten the check, so I went back to the bank, where they told me they don't know what happened to the Letter of Instruction I'd sent, so I had to fill out another one, get it notarized again, and resend it to the same address.

Which I did.

But three months after that, I still hadn't gotten the check.

So I called the bank, and the woman told me that they didn't know what happened to the second Letter of Instruction I sent, either. She told me to come back a third time, get a third Letter of Instruction, get it notarized a third time, and send it to the same address.

In other words, I'm POD but it's been over a year since Mother Mary passed. Put simply, there has been D, but there is still no P.

So I told the bank lady what I thought of that, in creatively profane terms.

Because I am my mother's daughter.

And I have no reason to believe that the fourth time I do the same thing will lead to success.

In fact, it was Albert Einstein who said, "Insanity: doing the same thing over and over again and expecting different results."

Guy was a genius.

I wish I knew where he banks.

I know where he doesn't.

Bank of Insanity.

Anyway, you don't have to be Einstein to know that I will have to do what the bank says, all over again, for the fourth time. The bank has the money, and they've had it for over a year, and they're keeping it, even though it's not theirs anymore.

If they do this to enough people, they'll have free use of lots of money.

And they'll get away with it, because banks run America.

And the federal banking laws are basically, what's mine is mine, and what's yours is mine.

If you don't think so, try to be even a week late on your credit-card payment, mortgage, or car loan. You'll be charged late fees and interest, and you'll get threatening phone calls from the Mafia.

I mean, the banks.

I'm writing about it because I know I'm not the only person to lose a beloved parent, which is bad enough, but banks make it all worse by their pointless rules, red tape, and general incompetence, which only serve to remind you that YOUR MOM DIED.

You know what Mother Mary would say, don't you?

I do, too.

And that's why she will never really D.

A Thing of Beauty
FRANCESCA

"Beauty is truth, truth beauty, — that is all
Ye know on earth, and all ye need to
   know."

Keats, one of the greatest poets of the Romantic era.

I once wrote an entire term paper on those lines, and I still didn't understand them.

Aesthetic pleasure isn't completely lost on me; I've always dated attractive people. But I've mostly found my level. I don't think my looks are my best trait, which I'm perfectly fine with, so I've never prioritized that in my romantic partners.

But if you look at the great literature of the past, so much ink has been spilled for beauty. Such artistic depth for such a superficial subject. I didn't get it.

Until I dated someone super hot.

Remember that guy I met at the bachelorette party? His dance moves won me over that night, and it was a little too dark to get a great look at him. Then it took two months of playful texting before we could get our schedules to sync up. So when we finally made plans for a first date, I'd practically forgotten what he looked like.

We were meeting at a Lower East Side speakeasy, one of those kitschy bars with a hidden entrance. He texted me that he would wait outside and added, "I'm the one in orange."

I remember thinking he had to be pretty bold to pull off orange on a first date.

Then I spotted him.

He was gorgeous by every superficial metric possible. He was taller than I'd remembered, at least six-foot-three, and perfectly proportioned with broad shoulders tapering to a trim waist. Da Vinci's *Vitruvian Man* would look awkward beside him.

He wore a pumpkin-colored, fine-knit sweater that draped over his pectoral muscles and strained at his biceps.

I would've undressed him with my eyes, but I'd never seen someone that fit naked in real life.

I had to use my imagination.

Then he saw me and flashed a dazzling smile.

And I wanted to throw up.

I plunged into an abyss of insecurity. As we hugged hello, a million thoughts ran through my head: Was my dress flattering? I should suck in. I had rushed my eyeliner, was it uneven? I forgot leg moisturizer. I should've worn less perfume. Am I wearing deodorant? Yes, but not enough.

"You found me," he said. "My buddy said I look like a traffic cone."

He could certainly stop traffic.

"You look . . . great."

Where's poetry when you need it?

We went inside and sat at the bar. As we talked, my eyes traced the outlines of his face by candlelight. His bone structure made the Parthenon look amateurish, he had the cheekbones of a god, a jawline cut from marble, and these full, pillowy lips made for, well . . .

Where was that drink?

I tried to focus on the words coming out of his mouth, but my mind was busy comparing myself to the type of girl he typically dates.

He was saying, "Well, I have four brothers . . ."

The girl he dates styles her hair every morning, and she knows how to do that soft-wave thing with a curling iron. I don't even own a curling iron. My stupid hair is

241

already curly.

"One year we were on the football team at the same time . . ."

She probably loves running, she runs on vacation. She used to be a gymnast. Or a ballerina. Or play collegiate beach volleyball — is that a thing?

". . . new job, it's not the usual finance . . ."

She has never had a pimple, but she heard of them, and they sound awful.

". . . What year were you?"

Shit. Focus — what was he saying? You two went to the same college so . . .

"I was class of '08," I said. A lucky guess.

"That's why we never met, I was 2011." He paused. "But, I've always dated older women."

Twenty-nine years old and already I was the older woman. This did not boost my confidence.

I told myself that now that he has seen me in the light of day, he would recognize that we're different categories of human and return to dating the girls Derek Jeter or Leonardo DiCaprio had just dumped. Reassured that this ordeal was our first and last date, I started to relax and enjoy it.

I learned that he played football in college and was an avid Patriots fan. He deduced from my hometown that I might be an angry Eagles fan.

"I plead the Fifth," I said. "I'm trying to get you to like me."

"You don't have to worry about that. I like you."

He put his hand on my leg. I stared at it.

The audio of him saying, "I like you," echoed in my mind in slow motion.

I floated home.

But dating someone so good-looking was a roller coaster for my self-esteem. The first few times, I still believed he was out of my league. I got ready for dates like I was getting ready for prom, deploying all my makeup tricks until I was basically wearing an Instagram filter on my face.

Although I will say, I gained a new understanding of taking artistic inspiration in beauty. Over the next few weeks, I caught myself sketching his perfect face. In one drawing, I captured him quite well. I briefly considered texting him a picture of it.

Thankfully, I thought better of it.

In the modern dating world where speaking on the phone is too intimate, sending someone a portrait you drew of him is equivalent to sending a bloody ear.

But when a few more dates proved the "I like you" comment wasn't a hallucination sent by the Muses, it started to go to my head.

Was I secretly stunning? Maybe I had a rare beauty that had not been properly appreciated until this moment. I'd been selling myself short all this time. I was a ten in six's clothing.

The next time we went out, I wore a crop top.

I was drunk with power.

He'd suggested we go dancing to reprise our first meeting. That Studly Do Right wanted to do something so sentimental had me convinced we were fated to be together. I was already imagining our genetic-lottery-winning children scampering around together.

And we had a great time. We chatted over rosé before going downstairs where a DJ was spinning nineties hip-hop, and we danced the night away. People were looking at us, we were such a hot couple.

See how quickly I'd transitioned to "we"?

At around 1 A.M., we went back upstairs to get some air. It was the first date with him that I hadn't felt like a total mess. I thought I had played it perfectly.

"Oh, my friend just texted me," he said. "They're in Meatpacking. Want to meet them at a club?"

A club in the Meatpacking District? A friend? This was all wrong. I was ready to go home. With him.

But I couldn't cop to being tired. Exhaustion is for old, ugly people.

We arrived at 1 Oak, the clubbiest of clubs. The next three hours were a blur of strobe lighting, smoke machines, and very, very overpriced bottles of Grey Goose.

I gave it the old college try. I drank vodka–Red Bulls, a disgusting cocktail that tastes like Mountain Dew concentrate. I tried to dance without choking from the smoke machine. And I made friends with a group of drag queens, because they struck me as the most authentic women in the room.

One thing was clear: hot or not, I was too old for this.

At five in the morning, I got my wish and went home with the hottest guy in the room.

Where we slept on top of my covers, fully clothed.

He woke up at eight thirty, bright-eyed and handsome as ever. I woke up with a hangover that felt like the afterlife.

Still, waking up with a deadly hangover next to him was better than alone.

Emily Dickinson, another Romantic poet and fellow spinster writer, put it well: "If I expire, let it be in sight of thee."

We went out a few more times, but in the end, we fizzled out. I can't say a bad thing about him, but we were missing some secret ingredient to make us fall in love.

It turns out looks aren't everything.

Percy Bysshe Shelley, a poet who'd been married twice by my age, got it: "Love, hope, and self-esteem, like clouds depart."

Finding someone incredibly attractive doesn't guarantee a connection between two souls.

But it does give you something to write about.

OVER TROUBLED WATERS

LISA

I just got back from book tour with Daughter Francesca, which was wonderful except for one thing:

Bridges.

As in, I'm newly scared of driving over them.

Please tell me I'm not alone.

We were touring for our book titled *Does This Beach Make Me Look Fat?*, so our publisher scheduled us for a book tour of bookstores in beach resorts, and I'm not complaining. But I knew I was in trouble on day one, as I drove toward Rehoboth, encountering my first bridge. It rose ahead of me like a concrete tsunami, and all of a sudden, I felt weak in the knees.

And not good weak-in-the-knees, like Bradley Cooper weak-in-the-knees.

More like squeeze your sphincter weak-in-the-knees.

In other words, the wrong kind of puckering up.

The bridge was the Chesapeake & Delaware Canal Bridge, and even though it was new, it looked unfinished. It didn't have a top or any structure to hold it up, but only weird spikes that rose in the center, attached to things that looked like strings.

I own bras with more support.

The other problem was that the bridge didn't have any sides. As we got closer, I imagined sliding right off into the water, which I admit might have been irrational, or a big tractor-trailer behind me pushing me off, which seemed completely likely.

Francesca looked over, worried. "Mom, are you okay?"

"Of course I'm okay," I lied, because I'm a good mother.

A good mother doesn't communicate her irrational fears to her child.

A good mother lets her child develop her own irrational fears.

But as we drove onto the bridge, the more nervous I got, and Francesca could tell. "Mom, why are your knees shaking? Are you thinking about Bradley Cooper again?"

So I confessed that I was afraid of the bridge, and being the great daughter that she is, she didn't tease me, but turned into my cheerleader/therapist.

"Mom, just keep your foot on the gas and follow the car ahead of you, and we'll be fine."

We got over the bridge without lethal event, but my heart was thumping. I cursed the bridge, its architects, and my hormones in general, because I remember reading somewhere that fear of bridges can be correlated to estrogen levels.

Unfortunately, I'm fresh out.

The only liquid I have in great supply is Diet Coke.

Our book tour took us to independent bookstores in Avalon, Westhampton, Mystic, and Westerly, Rhode Island, which meant we crossed about three thousand bridges, or maybe it just felt that way. I was a wreck, and Francesca took over the driving, which only made me more nervous.

What mother isn't nervous when her kid drives?

I braced myself in the passenger seat, and Francesca said I looked like a starfish.

Plus I still had to close my eyes when we went over a bridge, whether I was driving or not, and by the end of book tour, I had become a full-fledged Nervous Driver. All around me, traffic moved way too fast. Speed limits have increased from fifty-five to sixty-five, which means that everybody goes seventy to seventy-five. Cars changed lanes willy-nilly, passed on the right, and even drove on the shoulder.

I-95 isn't a highway, it's a video game.

And next week, Francesca and I have a wedding in Newport, a route that goes over the Claiborne Pell Bridge.

Which is the longest suspension bridge in New England.

This starfish is flying.

PARTY HEARTY

LISA

Happiness is a warm puppy.

I didn't make that up.

I just believed it, and somehow I ended up with five dogs.

Which stopped being puppies way too fast.

Although they still leave the occasional present on the rug.

I've learned that housebroken is a misnomer.

Your dogs don't end up broken for the house.

Your house ends up broken for the dogs.

Or at best, the house starts to smell, more and more each year, but after a while, you stop noticing. People entering your home for the first time will ask, Is something dying in here?

And you will answer, Yes.

I am.

Anyway, I bring this up because I've read that there's a new company in Brooklyn that will rent you puppies for parties.

The cost is a few hundred dollars.

Which proves that there's a chew toy born every minute.

The company's specialty is renting you puppies for your child's birthday party.

Which makes perfect sense, because we all know children love puppies.

For thirty seconds.

The company also rents puppies for a Student Stress-Relief Puppy Party, a Sweet 16 Puppy Party, and a Corporate Puppy Party.

For corporate puppies.

You could also have a Quinceañeras Puppy Party, at which you can teach your puppy to sit, stay, and pronounce Quinceañeras.

Good luck.

The company is not called Party Poopers.

But it should be.

Anyway, I think this is an excellent idea.

In fact, I want to get in on the fun.

And the money.

For a small fee, I will happily rent you my dogs. I will drop them off at your house for an hour. They will bring presents and leave them on the rug.

They will break your house for you.

Okay, I take that back.

I will pay you to take my dogs for a few hours.

You name the price.

In a related story, I read that there's a company in California that will rent you reptiles for your party. Some of the reptiles included are snakes, iguanas, turtles, monitors, frogs, toads, bugs, and lizards.

If this sounds like a plague that you pay for, it might be.

I don't want a reptile in my house.

It reminds me too much of my second marriage.

I didn't need a divorce lawyer.

I needed an exterminator.

Also a fumigator.

And an exorcist.

Pet rental must be a thing, because I read that there are restaurants popping up in California, called Dog and Cat Cafés, where you can eat a meal among dogs and cats.

I live in the dog and cat café.

But I never get to leave.

I think these companies are onto something.

And I was imagining things I could rent out for parties and make some dough.

For example, most of the women I know are middle-aged, which is the new term for sixty-year-olds.

Have you heard that seventy is the new twenty?

Take it from me, it is.

Or it will be until I turn seventy, when eighty will be the new twenty.

However, not all of us are ready to be grandmothers, and not all of our children are ready to be parents.

So what's the answer?

I might start renting out babies for parties.

I could just drop off a bunch of babies at your house and you could kiss and hug them for a few hours.

They could leave you presents, too.

Post-Menopausal Parties!

Bring your own eggs!

We could make Estrogen Replacementinis!

No?

Okay, instead I could rent out a bunch of handymen for your party. I could drop off a carpenter, an electrician, a painter, and a plumber at your house and pick them up an hour later.

Now we're talking.

Honestly, between a handyman and a baby, every woman I know would take the handyman.

And we're all mothers.

In fact, between a handyman and a male stripper, every woman I know would take the handyman.

That's why I think it's so funny when male strippers dress up like handymen.

They think we're fantasizing about sex.

We're really fantasizing about a new bookshelf.

And a house where everything that's broken gets fixed.

Even the dogs.

Rings of Love
FRANCESCA

Last weekend, I got to be a bridesmaid in my best friend's wedding, and I loved every minute of it.

I was so excited to be included, all summer I had to stop myself from calling it "our wedding." I loved seeing her try on gowns, I loved the bachelorette party, I loved the bridal shower.

I even loved my bridesmaid dress.

I'm a really good friend.

I did everything except diet with her.

I'm not *that* good a friend.

The wedding weekend itself was full of spectacular events, ramping up in order of magnificence. And when the big day arrived, it was more beautiful than anything I could've imagined.

And I didn't mess up! I gave a heartfelt, if inebriated, speech at the rehearsal dinner. I did not trip and fall when we processed down the aisle.

I did accidentally sit on her veil when we were getting ready, but nobody saw.

All told, she got hitched without a hitch.

At the reception, I gave the bride space to spend time with her guests and enjoy the few breathers alone with her groom. With the pre-wedding events, especially the epic bridal party primping session that had begun at 10 A.M., I'd gotten a lot of girl-time with her.

So I scanned the dance floor looking for other friends to boogie with, and I spotted my best guy friend from childhood.

We've always had each other's backs on the dance floor, whether I was making sure he had someone to slow-dance with in seventh grade, or when he rescued me from going to the senior prom alone after my boyfriend dumped me a week before.

He's not a friend, he's a brother.

As we broke it down to Beyoncé, same as we had back when she was in Destiny's Child, it struck me how surreal it was that we found ourselves together that night.

In a twist of fate, he was invited because his fiancée is the bride's best friend from childhood, and we introduced them.

Not only that, this very wedding might not have happened if we hadn't introduced them, because his fiancée was returning the matchmaking favor when she introduced the bride to the groom!

We're better than Tinder.

I shouted to him over the music, "Do you realize, we've been friends eighteen years?"

"Since sixth grade, baby!"

"And in three weeks, we'll be dancing at your wedding!"

"I know, it's crazy."

But maybe it isn't that crazy. Maybe this is how it's supposed to work.

One good heart tossed into the world ripples out to embrace other good-hearted people.

Love multiplies.

And each outer ring protects the inner ones.

I didn't see that before. Amidst all my excitement about my best friend's wedding, I had a little apprehension, too. Not that I'd lose her — we studied abroad in college together, which ensures lifelong friendship, by blackmail at the very least — but apprehension that things might change.

Come to think of it, I had the same apprehension when my guy friend and I graduated high school and left for college six hundred miles apart.

And yet, here we are, friends old and new, tighter than ever.

Change can be a good thing, despite the bad press it gets, and even close friendships have room to grow outward. It'd be too hard for one person to gather enough people to love all on their own. It's a group effort. And the whole is greater than the sum of its parts.

At the end of the night, all the guests lined up on either side of the long entrance hall for the grand send-off of the bride and groom. We cheered and snapped pictures and shook tambourines as the newlyweds scampered down the aisle, laughing and waving on their way to their getaway car.

I blew them a kiss that I'm not sure they saw. But that twinge of melancholy at seeing my best friend wave good-bye and disappear into the limo lasted only a moment.

Yes, she's about to embark on a new phase of her life. And yes, my role in her life may change. But as time goes on and our hearts grow more rings, we don't have to leave anyone behind. We can hold on to each other, and collect new hearts to hold, from this day forward, as long as we all shall live.

THANKS FOR ASKING!
LISA

I feel so loved.

By corporate entities.

It begins Saturday night after I come home from having gone to a movie with my Bestie Franca. I open my computer and there's an email from Fandango:

"Lisa, did you enjoy *Mission Impossible: Rogue Nation*?"

Aw, how nice of you to ask, Fandango!

The email also asked, "How many stars would you give the movie? Do you want to rate it?"

I didn't rate it, but I give it five stars. Tom Cruise is at his Tom Cruisiest, this time with a strong female heroine.

Who should be me, but isn't.

Never mind that I can't shoot a gun, drive a motorcycle, or wear liquid eyeliner.

Then I got another email, this time from Trip Advisor, an app that Francesca and I used on our book tour:

"Lisa, how did you enjoy Mystic, Connecticut? Do you want to post a comment?"

Well, I did like Mystic, Connecticut, but I hadn't known Trip Advisor cared so much. And I didn't want to post a comment because I didn't feel as excited about Mystic, Connecticut, as I did about *Mission Impossible: Rogue Nation*.

And really, who has the time to post a comment? I had to get back to answering my email from all the other companies that were totally in love with me.

I had an email from Yelp, an app that Francesca and I had used to find a restaurant on tour:

"Lisa, did you enjoy your meal at Elvira's Pancake House?"

Yes, and thank you for reminding me that I cheated on my diet. My jeans are telling me the same thing, so you two might be in cahoots.

Later I got an email from Amazon because I had recently bought research books online:

"Lisa, did you enjoy *The Serial Killer Files*?"

Frankly, I enjoyed *The Serial Killer Files* as much as you can enjoy a book about serial killers, but it's my job to read the occasional book about serial killers, so I'm not complaining.

Thanks for asking, Amazon!

You may remember the good old days, when you came home and somebody asked you, "How was your day?"

And in response, you answered by telling them about your day, though you did not rate it, assign it one-to-five stars, or post a comment online.

I seem to recall this is called conversation.

It usually occurs face-to-face over a dinner table, but it also occurs on the telephone, in which case it takes much longer and usually devolves into a conversation about dogs, carbohydrates, or back pain.

So it's not really the worst thing in the world that corporate entities ask us the same question.

I think of them like our corporate friends and family.

And like our friends and family, they often ask us to help. They want us to recommend restaurants, movies, or books, so that more people will use their website, and they can make a living.

I don't begrudge them that. Because I love them back.

However, I have learned to be wary of online reviews, because people tend to be harsh, especially in book reviews. You could write the Bible, and there would still be people who post:

"I give it one star. Not enough action."

Or, "I give it one star. Too much action."

I don't rely on online movie reviews either, because they can be quirky. I've loved movies that got a low rating on Rotten Tomatoes, and I've hated movies that got high ratings. Once, Bestie Franca and I walked out of a movie that had gotten a 98 percent rating. We got so bored waiting for something to happen that we made something happen.

We left.

I don't post reviews of anything I don't like, and I review only things I like. The same is true when I review a book for a newspaper. I always remember that there's an actual human being at the receiving end. I follow that old-school motto, If you don't have something nice to say, don't say anything at all.

However, my beloved Mother Mary followed Dorothy Parker's motto, which was, "If you don't have anything nice to say, come sit by me."

So we differ.

Why am I the way I am?

Because life is too short.

And at the end, I wonder if we'll all get

one last email:
 "Lisa, how did you enjoy your life?"

LOOKING AT MY GARDEN
LISA

This is the time of year that gardeners hate.

Or at least, this gardener.

It's mid-October, and the leaves on the trees are turning gorgeous reds, oranges, and yellow.

Unfortunately, my garden is turning brown and black, and I scan it sadly.

The bee balm has dried into black pom-poms, like a cluster of punctuation marks.

The day lilies that used to be a vibrant yellow have closed their leaves like a bankrupt business.

The groundcover is the same color as the ground.

The milkweed has morphed into weird pods that remind me of a science-fiction movie.

The rosebushes have succumbed to the Japanese beetles who ate their leaves, making them as fragile as my ex's ego.

God knows where that thought came from.

An ex-husband is the gift that keeps on giving, and every woman should have at least one.

Even if your life is happy and peaceful, like mine is, and your thoughts are walking along, like mine were, you can catch yourself stepping into a puddle of bile and resentment, like unexpectedly wet ground, so that when you're looking at a garden you used to love, which has now turned to complete crap, you find yourself thinking, "Oh, I remember him."

By the way, I'm not talking about Thing One. I'm talking about Thing Two.

I'm always talking about Thing Two, for the simple reason that Daughter Francesca is the offspring of Thing One, so there is at least one good reason I don't regret that marriage.

I can't say the same for Thing Two.

I can't say a single nice thing about Thing Two.

And though I haven't seen the man in ages, nor do I have any contact with him whatsoever, I still find myself remembering bits and pieces of weird things, and I think, Why did I put up with that? How could I have been so stupid? Why did I waste so much time, energy, and money?

So you see, this story started out being about a garden and was about to segue into the seasons of the year, but has now turned into the seasons of a woman's life, not all of which were deliriously happy.

Other women talk about the One Who Got Away, meaning a man whom they loved and regret losing.

But my One Who Got Away was a man whom I loved and regret not killing.

Too dark?

Just kidding.

Kind of.

It's the kind of thought that sneaks up on you, and now that I've gotten older and seen winter turn into spring and back again more than sixty times, I know that life is full of light and dark, and it's okay to acknowledge both.

I'm not falling back on that old cliché that you need the dark to appreciate the light, because frankly, I'm not sure that's completely true.

I feel blessed and lucky every day.

I wake up feeling grateful, merely because I woke up.

You don't have to read the obituaries to know that life is a gift.

I know when a good thing is happening

just because it feels so terrific, and there's more than one time I've said to myself, Remember this great feeling, because this is as good as it gets.

I felt that way when Francesca was born.

I felt that way when Francesca took her first step, and when she graduated high school, then college.

I feel that way every time she and I are laughing together about some memory, or something goofy that we both do, or saying to each other what we call our audio "drops," our shared language of phrases we remember from movies we've loved, some twenty years old.

I also feel that way when I meet one of my readers at a signing, and I even feel that way when I get an email from one of them, saying that they enjoyed my book or that it got them through a hard time in their life, the illness of a loved one or their own chemotherapy.

I feel that way about my friends, and the editor of this very book.

I'm grateful for the people in my life.

I feel that way every time I hug one of my dogs, or when they wag their tails, or when they lick my face in the morning.

I feel that way anytime I'm riding Buddy, my paint pony, who at the age of thirty-two, has seen the seasons of life himself.

I even feel that way about my cat Vivi, who sheds gray fur across my legs, which luckily matches my sweatpants.

I'm grateful for the animals in my life.

And I feel that way when I take a walk and look around at the countryside.

Nature evokes feelings of gratitude and grace, even as the leaves turn color and fall away.

So it's only the blackness of my dead garden that reminds me of my second marriage.

It's my own personal punctuation mark, my little black hole of negative emotion.

Permit me my dark places.

Maybe you have them, too. Maybe you don't.

Whether they do us good or not, I don't like to pretend bad feelings away.

I'd rather prove I've moved past them.

After all, everything casts a shadow.

But the great thing about a shadow?

You get to leave it behind.

Pop Goes the Pill
LISA

More advancements in medical research, to benefit women!

The hits just keep on coming, don't they?

I'm talking about a banner week in women's health, in which two news stories were only apparently unrelated.

The first news story concerns a breakthrough for women, in that modern medical science has developed a pill to increase our libido.

Thank God!

This development obviously counters all those critics who say that modern medicine does not devote enough time to women's health.

Here's your answer, ladies, a pill to increase your sexual desire!

By the way, there is no pill yet that will cure breast cancer, ovarian cancer, or a variety of other life-threatening illnesses that women get. Nor is there a pill to cure any other cancer or illness that both women and men get. There is however, a pill to increase male sexual desire and a pill to increase female desire.

Which should teach you, above all, that sex sells.

Drug companies know this, and I guess a few people have to die so that a few others can have sex more frequently.

Honestly, it's a small price to pay, isn't it?

At least for the people having sex.

I'm not one of those people, as loyal readers may know.

And since I'm not having sex, I don't really miss it.

I'm here to tell you, if you don't use it, you do lose it.

But the real truth is, you don't miss it.

In fact, I hadn't realized that I had an illness that needed curing until they came up with a pill.

Which puts me in an unusual position.

No, not that position.

Get your mind out of the gutter.

My problem is I'm too busy to miss sex.

And I don't think I'm the only middle-aged woman who feels this way.

I've been writing, reading, riding bicycles, playing with my dogs, trying to get my cats to love me, pulling out weeds, going to movies with my friends, and generally enjoying my life.

What am I supposed to do?

Take a pill so that I don't have any fun anymore?

Who will finish writing my novel? Who will weed my garden? Who will be rejected by my cats?

It's a pill that poses problems for single women, namely, where do you find a man to meet your pharmaceutically enhanced needs?

This would be the sexual equivalent of being all dressed up with nowhere to go.

Especially if you take the pill and then start prowling, which could make you vaguely desperate, and we all know how much men love that.

But I'm thinking the solution to the problem came in another news story this week, that of Ashley Madison. You may have heard that Ashley Madison is a website for married men and women to cheat on each other, but a recent hacking exposed that the website has about 3 billion men registered and only twenty women.

I could've told you that.

Women are too busy reading novels, weeding gardens, walking dogs, and enjoying their lives to go on a stupid website like Ashley Madison.

Plus women are too smart to enjoy hook-up sex, and no pill is going to cure them of that.

You know why?

Because there's nothing wrong with them.

It ain't broke, so it doesn't need fixing.

I don't like the idea of a pill that makes you want something you didn't otherwise want.

I don't know why you would take it, unless your man is taking one, too, and he wants you to want what he wants.

He probably wouldn't want it either, if he weren't taking a pill.

So maybe it's time to stop popping pills to make us pop.

God might've intended everybody to cool their jets in middle age.

Look at nature. Even the moon isn't full all the time.

To everything there is a season, and can't we all just slow our roll?

Isn't anything allowed to wane in our youth-obsessed, nipped-and-tucked, filled-and-injected culture? Must we look and act like we're twenty-five, until we keel over dead?

I think we should mellow out and enjoy our lives, and if we're lucky enough, enjoy the company of whomever you love. If you feel like hopping in the sack, great. If you don't, go walk the dog.

Intimacy takes many forms.

Talk to each other.

Read to each other.

Weed together.

In fact, come to my house and weed my garden, you crazy kids.

Now that's my idea of a threesome.

THOSE WHO CAN'T DATE, SET UP

FRANCESCA

One of my best guy friends is the most eligible man I know — he's successful, brilliant, handsome, funny, and gay.

Damn it.

After a decade of friendship, I should be used to that last one, but it makes me mad every time. To quell my disappointment that I can't date him myself, I've taken to playing matchmaker for him.

Those who can't date, set up.

And although I've found him some pretty great guys, I think I've gotten more out of the process than he has.

Every woman can learn from playing wing-woman for her gay guy friend.

It's good for everyone's love karma to help potential couples find each other. But I've found that a good set-up is a little problematic with my heterosexual friends.

For instance, I'm always skeptical when one of my single, straight girlfriends wants to set me up with a guy she knows. I usually accept, but the entire first date I'm consumed with trying to figure out why she didn't want to date him herself.

It's like the opposite of a treasure hunt.

Red-flag football.

This ethical quandary is why I can't often set up my girlfriends. I'm single myself, and if I meet a terrific single guy, I want him. And if I don't want him, there's probably something wrong with him that would disqualify him for my friends.

I only make matches in good faith.

Setting up my straight-guy friends is difficult in a different way. I do have a few male pals who are terrific people, friend-zoned by fate, whom I would love to see happy with someone. But straight men are just so hard to read. Whenever I set up a straight male friend with a girl, this happens:

If he liked her, he'll tell me, "She was great!" and call her again.

If he didn't like her, he'll tell me, "She was great!" and never call her again.

So 50 percent of the time, the girl comes to me upset and confused, and I can't give her any info. Plus, I've learned nothing about my friend's taste to improve the algorithm and make a better match next time.

Cupid Fail.

I think the problem lies in that my straight male friends aren't comfortable criticizing a date, because they'd fear — or know — that I'd identify with the woman. He'd never just tell me he didn't like her body, or she talked too much. It's too awkward to discuss.

I probably wouldn't understand their reasons anyway.

"You didn't like her? But did you see her adorable shoes? She has amazing EQ!"

And I'm crap at guessing at women's attractiveness, because I'm not sexually attracted to them.

Look, if I knew the key to heterosexual dating, I wouldn't be single.

My gay friend offers me matchmaking redemption. It turns out, when I'm not considering a man for myself, I'm way better at evaluating them as a potential mate. My friend tells me I consistently recommend his most quality suitors.

Take that, Tinder.

And although my aim was truly altruistic, I've learned a ton about myself in helping him out. Our opposite genders but mutual attraction to men has provided ideal test conditions for me to identify my own romantic neuroses.

Lesson 1: Don't be afraid to toss back a

good fish.

One time I set up my friend with a guy I thought would be a slam-dunk. He had an education dripping in Ivy, a job in finance but interest in the creative arts, funny but not funnier than my friend, and he looked like he walked out of J.Crew's fall catalog.

They don't make straight men like this.

My friend liked him, but he didn't love him. He said there was some chemistry missing. Close, but no cigar.

He didn't obsess over it, he just trusted his gut.

I think of this when I'm trying to talk myself into another guy just because, objectively, he's a "catch." Love, of course, isn't objective, it's the most subjective force in the world. The notion that just any good guy would spell "Happily Ever After" for every girl is insane.

And yet women get pressure to deny their gut feelings all the time. We hear, "Don't be picky," or, "Let a nice guy win."

How many rom-com plots follow this narrative: girl hates boy, girl learns her lesson, girl settles for boy.

We don't trust our female leads to choose wisely, so why would we trust ourselves?

But my gay friend doesn't carry that sexist baggage. Watching him let go of a great guy who wasn't great for him has reminded me to trust my gut.

Lesson 2: Sometimes the kindest thing is not to go out again.

My next find for him was a man who was funny, smart, and kind — just like my friend. I thought their personalities were well-matched and encouraged them to meet.

They did, and afterwards my friend reported back at brunch. He said I was exactly right about the date's great personality — but, unfortunately, he just wasn't physically attracted, so he wouldn't be seeing him again.

He told me the guy had texted him that he was going to be back in the city the following weekend, but my friend replied only, "Have a nice trip."

"Ouch, that's cold," I said.

My friend shrugged. "The attraction issue isn't going to change. Better not to string him along."

He's right.

My girlfriends and I often talk about how every guy leaves a date with us thinking he knocked it out of the park, regardless of how we really felt about them. But is that really so "nice"? Without meaning to mislead anyone, I reflexively hide my feelings of disinterest. I would never want to be rude to a date, but my people-pleasing tendencies probably cause more confusion than necessary.

The next time I'm "just not that into" him, I won't feel guilty about declining date number two.

Which leads me to our next lesson.

Lesson 3: It's okay to be a little superficial.

Straight or gay, men understand this. A big part, but not all, of sexual attraction is undeniably physical. Men don't apologize for that, and no one expects them to.

"Men are visual" is the common phrase.

But women have eyes, too.

They're up here.

Some men get angry at women who have the gall to be turned off by something. Catcallers and Internet trolls alike can spend hours evaluating women's bodies, but the minute that attraction isn't reciprocated, she's a "stuck-up bitch."

It's the *Beauty and the Beast* model. If the guy likes you, the only nice thing to do is like him back.

I've internalized the idea that virtuous women aren't supposed to care about looks. I feel so guilty when I'm not attracted to an otherwise-nice guy. I usually give him three dates and pray he'll grow on me.

But would Beast have loved Belle if she

didn't look drop-dead gorgeous in a yellow dress? I don't remember anyone suggesting Beast just aim lower and find true love with another beast.

Women have to stop indulging these double standards and punishing ourselves for human nature if we're going to find love outside of a fairytale.

So I'm learning. With each set-up attempt, I feel I'm getting closer and closer to finding a partner wonderful enough for the best man I know.

And without meaning to, I might figure out how to better find one for myself.

EMPTY NESTING FOR EXPERTS

LISA

Before I continue, let me make one thing clear.

I love my daughter Francesca.

This is, by now, a matter of record.

I've said it about a million times and written essays about it.

I give this very obvious preamble because I don't want you to misconstrue the following.

Which is that I really love being an empty-nester.

I wasn't sure I would feel this way. I was worried about Francesca's moving out, especially because I was a single mother most of my life, and so it's just been the two of us in the house, with way too many dogs, cats, fish, and guinea pigs.

And that's just the animals we kept in the house.

I was worried about how I would deal with the change in my life when I was on my own, and wrote about that in one of our earlier volumes, which was titled *My Nest Isn't Empty, It Just Has More Closet Space.*

That was published when Francesca was just about to fly the coop, and I will tell you secretly that the title was aspirational. I was cheering myself up, unsure about how I was going to face the future.

I think you might be familiar with doing that.

Women are terrific at putting a brave face on things.

We turn that frown upside down like nobody's business.

Not that we hide our feelings, but we try to be strong for everybody, and that's part of our job as mothers.

If your bond with your children is strong, which I suspect it is because you're reading this, then you may have done the same thing.

We're the leaders of the family, though we don't always put it that way. I always thought of it that way. We set the tone for the family and the house exactly the same way that a CEO sets a corporate culture. Your house can feel happy and stable or miserable and dramatic, depending not on events but on how a mother reacts to the events.

You cannot keep adversity from your life or protect your children from hardship. These things will come, and they should, because how you handle them will teach your child how to handle them. A child will always take a cue from its mother.

I lived that, so I know.

But that was then, and this is now.

I love my daughter, but I absolutely love being an empty-nester.

It's been over five years since she moved to Manhattan, and I can't tell you how great it is to have complete and total freedom to do whatever I want, whenever I please.

In fact, I've gotten dangerously used to it.

My days are still busy, writing and doing whatever business things that are associated with my books, as well as answering emails and going online to post on Facebook, Twitter, and Instagram, usually about my books, but more often about my dogs.

They love publicity.

I take videos of them, and also the horses and chickens, having the time of my life. Sometimes I realize that I'm doing these things to reach out to people, to let them into my life because I like that connection, but even that is on my terms. It's not as if I have to pick anybody up after play practice, run to the store to make sure there's food for dinner, or bang on the door at Staples after closing time, so I can buy whatever supplies we need for some last-minute school project.

I don't have to get up early to make anybody's lunch.

I can put the TV on whatever channel I want to, at whatever volume I want to.

I can watch TV late at night, having a little party with James Corden, who's terrific.

I can ride my pony whenever I want to, and the same with walking the dogs.

There are a million little things that every day keep me busy and active, and I never worry about filling the time, because I need so much more of it than a mere twenty-four hours.

But in a good way.

And when I reflect upon my happiness of late, I don't think it has to do with any of those quotidian freedoms, as joyful as they are.

I think it has to do with something bigger, which is that now I no longer have responsibility for another human being under my roof.

I don't have to lead anybody anymore.

I'm CEO in a company of exactly one.

I have only myself to take care of these days.

And that is glorious.

A child is a beloved responsibility.

But a responsibility just the same.

When I talk to my fellow empty-nesters, I find that we are generally deliriously happy, and I hear them expressing the same general feeling.

We used to be afraid that when that responsibility was lifted, there would be absence, a loss, or an empty hole, or a general lack thereof.

Ladies, I assure you, that isn't the case.

Nature abhors a vacuum, and so do empty-nesters.

Your time will get filled up with everything, at the same time that your interests expand, your obligations narrow to just one thing.

You.

Enjoy.

EMPTY NESTING FOR EXPERTS, PART TWO
LISA

I'm skipping the preamble because you just read it, but remember I love my daughter Francesca when you read the following:

I love when she comes home to visit, but it is not without incident.

In other words, after you become an experienced empty-nester, you get used to the complete freedom you have and the many preferences you develop, which will be disturbed when your beloved daughter reenters your Mom Orbit.

Star Wars will not result, but there may be minor interplanetary skirmishes for which you should be prepared.

Like, for example, the fact that I like to watch CNN, twenty-four/seven.

Let me explain.

I don't actually *watch* TV because I'm working, but I like it on in the background during the daytime, and it is not easy to find daytime television that's not a soap opera, which would distract me with semi-nudity, or talk shows with celebrity interviews, which could distract me with Bradley Cooper.

Don't get me started.

And I admit with presidential politics in the air of late, I've gotten very interested in the news, so I like to stay tuned to a relatively neutral station like CNN.

I don't know your particular political orientation, but I keep an open mind and have voted both Republican and Democratic in my day. So if we assume that FOX is for Republicans and MSNBC is for Democrats, the only acronym we're left with is CNN.

Also I admit that since events in the Middle East have heated up, I've become more alarmed about the violence and war in the world, so I like to keep informed.

Just in case somebody drops a bomb on me.

I want to know it first.

"Why are you watching CNN?" Francesca asks, home for a visit.

I generally answer with the above.

Francesca frowns, not angrily, but out of concern for her extremely naïve mother. "They're just scaring you."

"No, they're informing me about scary things."

"Mom. They're exaggerating all of the threats, so you stay tuned. That's what they do." Francesca sits down at the kitchen island, and I stand on the opposite side where I always do, as if I am defending hearth, home, and The Way I Do Things Now That I'm an Empty-Nester.

"The threats are real. The Russians are flying planes into Syria. That could lead to a world war."

Francesca half-smiles. "That's just what they want you to think."

"Honey, at my age, nobody tells me what to think. I know what I think, I just like to stay informed."

"Okay, I get it." Francesca backs off, because she knows this is not worth getting into a fight over, but after dinner, which we eat at the kitchen island with CNN on, she starts frowning at the TV again. "Didn't we just see this show?"

"No, it's not the same show. This is live."

"But it's the same people. I recognize them from fifteen minutes ago."

"I know, it's the same people, but it's a different show. See in the corner, it says LIVE." I point to the screen, but even I know what she means. CNN spends all day talking with the same talking heads but shifting them in the chairs, like a shell game with political pundits.

"So it's the same people, saying the same things."

Still I defend my news station. I'm a loyal girl. "No, they're saying different things, and as new news comes in, they analyze it."

"But there is no new news. They're just massaging the old news, to keep you watching."

"Okay, maybe they are, but what if something new happens? I want to stay tuned."

Francesca rolls her eyes. "Nothing new is going to happen."

"You never know, with Syria."

I have a lot of opinions about Syria.

I'm all over Syria.

Syria doesn't make a move without my knowing.

I tell Francesca as much, and she laughs, but when we clear the dishes she starts frowning at the TV yet again.

"Mom, what's with the closed captioning?"

"I like it. I always keep it on."

"Why? Are you having trouble hearing?" Francesca's blue eyes narrow in a worried way. Exactly the way mine used to when Mother Mary showed signs of aging, and then, horribly, cancer.

The Flying Scottolines are nothing if not

dramatic. If the TV is on closed captioning, somebody might have cancer.

Ear cancer.

I shrug. "I can hear fine, I just like the closed captioning. Then I can just glance at the TV, or mute it, if I get a phone call."

"But the way you have it set up, the closed captioning takes up half the screen."

"True," I have to admit, "but there's nothing on the screen. Just the same people talking."

"Exactly!" Francesca says, as if she's won an argument we weren't having.

But I know who won.

Wolf Blitzer.

UNDEFINED

FRANCESCA

Labels have gotten a bad reputation. Labels lead to bullying, stifling a sense of self, inducing basic-ness. Labels in romantic relationships are deemed onerous by men, and the women who want them deemed needy and insecure. Cool girls don't need labels.

I had been seeing the European for several months, and I still had no idea what we were. However, this fit into his European profile. Only a lame American would want to know if we were Boyfriend & Girlfriend™. So I rolled with it.

Or tried to. I couldn't help but evaluate where we were headed. I analyzed the data as it came.

We would plan to see each other once a week without fail, often on prime weekend real estate. And each time, he took me on proper dates, with a meal and sometimes an activity.

Boyfriend material.

However, while we'd often have tentative plans for, say, Friday, he wouldn't text me to confirm any details until the eleventh hour, often forcing me to text him the humiliating "Are we still on?" at 6 P.M.

I hate the "Are we still on?" text.

Non-boyfriend material. Boyfriend by-product.

When we saw each other, he was attentive and engaged.

Boyfriend.

But in between our weekly dates, I hardly heard from him.

Not.

So, I was on the fence about him. But he was just handsome and accented enough for me to keep dating him from my fence.

My cool-girl façade began to crack the night we went to a holiday party of a mutual friend together. I thought we were going together — *together*-together — since we'd been dating for four months, and he had suggested we get dinner alone beforehand. I thought it would be our couple-coming-out party.

I mean, I got a blow-out for the occasion.

But after dinner, he insisted on buying his own bottle of wine to bring instead of letting mine count for both of us. This is the way they do it in Europe, he said.

Intimacy issues, imported.

When we arrived at the party, he took so long putting his jacket away that he effectively hid the fact that we had arrived at the same time. And after I assume he'd folded and color-sorted every single guest's coat, did he come to find me? No. Instead, he proceeded to make the rounds and talk to everyone but me.

Lest you think his inattention was all in my head, he left me so glaringly *available* that the host of the party, my pseudo-boyfriend's good pal, asked me out.

Clearly, the European hadn't mentioned he was seeing me.

This didn't feel Undefined.

This felt Single.

I tried to enjoy myself, but I was pissed. At the end of the night, I got my own coat to go.

Euro Trash materialized at my side. "You're leaving?"

"Yes, I'm tired," I answered as I said good-bye to other friends.

Unbidden, he followed me out and caught up with me on the sidewalk, linking an arm through mine. "Where are we going?"

"I'm going home."

"Well, am I coming with you?" He smiled slyly.

I stopped in my tracks. "Now you want to be with me? Because it didn't feel that way up there."

He apologized and explained he wasn't comfortable with PDA.

"I'm not suggesting we make out in the kitchen, I'm suggesting you stop acting like you're married."

Arguing on the street — trademark move of city romance.

Maybc we were in a relationship.

He vowed to be better at showing his feelings, and I forgave him. But it might have been that I didn't want to waste the blowout.

We got through the holidays, largely because he was overseas visiting family. But come January, I had grown tired of not knowing. We'd been undefined for five months. And something about the new year made me crave resolution.

Five months is too long for this basic American girl.

"Look, this is the longest I've ever dated someone without knowing where I stand."

"I know, and I'm sorry. It takes me longer to evaluate whether or not I want to be in a serious relationship than it does you."

Who said anything about being done evaluating? Dude, I'll be judging you all the way to the altar.

But instead I said, "If you need more time, that's okay. I'm not giving you an ultimatum."

Cool girl, see?

Cool, but not a doormat: "But in the meantime, I need you to show me that you care about me. I need to feel valued no matter what we are. And if you find yourself lukewarm, turn me loose. We can part ways with no hard feelings. Deal?"

He assured me that he cared "very much," that he wasn't seeing anyone else, and that he could see a "real future" with me.

One day at a time, bud.

As if the gods of love were delivering a test, that very night, I came down with the worst fever I've had in my adult life. I was so sick, I had to have him take me home early from our date. He made me tea and put me to bed.

Was this the new him showing me he cared? I wondered.

Then I didn't hear from him for two weeks.

So I had my answer.

When I'd regained my voice, I called him to break things off.

He said he was "blindsided," and that he's not the "type to do this over the phone."

I don't know what type he is, but I know my label for him.

Ex.

EVERYTHING OLD
IS NUDE AGAIN
LISA

You may have heard the bad news.

Playboy will no longer be publishing photos of nude women.

What's this world coming to?

Is nothing sacred?

Playboy has been around for as long as I've been alive, and I remember sneaking peeks at it when I went to babysit, because the people I babysat for kept theirs in the top drawer in their bedroom.

Don't ask me how I knew this.

Just take it from me that your babysitter knows more about your dresser drawers than you do.

By the way, I waited until the baby was asleep to start looking at pornography.

The very definition of a great babysitter.

This, back in the day when babysitters earned fifty cents an hour.

Listen, you get what you pay for.

Anyway, it should be obvious that a world

without *Playboy* magazine is the worst thing that can happen to women.

Without *Playboy,* how is a young girl going to learn that breasts should be at least a G cup?

To match a G-string.

It's sort of like matching your bra and your underwear, only different.

Not only that, but *Playboy* taught me that breasts are supposed to be completely devoid of moles, stretch marks, and nipple hair.

From now on, where are we going to get our self-loathing from?

You think it's easy to hate your body, overnight?

You need good reasons, and *Playboy* gave us tons of them.

Meanwhile, who else but *Playboy* would've ever thought of putting bunny ears and tails on women?

Who knew we could be woodland animals, as well as human beings?

Expanding our horizons!

Not only that, but *Playboy* was educational. It showed us women lots of interesting ways we could sit on hay bales, tractors, and even boring old beds. There's no reason to sit down and cross your legs, when you can lie down and form a flying wedge with whatever limbs you have available.

Open your mind, ladies.

And your legs!

Plus *Playboy* taught me about fashion, like the fact that I should match my outfits to my setting, so that anytime I sat on a hay bale, I knew that I was supposed to have a folksy-looking straw hat pulled down seductively over one eye.

Men are so into hats.

Also hay bales.

They love that.

Besides, I learned so much more from *Playboy* magazine, which was a true friend to women. For example, I used to read the hobbies of the various Playmates, and without that information, I never would've realized that walking on a beach could qualify as a hobby.

Good to know!

Come to think of it, I don't remember any of the Playmates saying that reading was her hobby.

Maybe the joke was on them, since people evidently stopped reading *Playboy*.

So I've clearly proven that life without *Playboy* will be terrible for women, but how would it be for men?

Just as bad.

How will young boys develop unrealistic

expectations of women?

You can't expect them to go back to *National Geographic*.

But wait, this just in.

The reason that *Playboy* isn't showing pictures of nude women anymore isn't because people aren't interested in pictures of nude women.

It's because there are so many free pictures of nude women on the Internet that *Playboy* can't make money that way anymore.

In other words, there are so many new businesses exploiting women that they are squeezing out the old businesses that used to exploit women.

The legacy exploiters aren't even being grandfathered in.

Explain that to your grandfather.

This is exactly the specter of technology that I've worried about.

That the Internet will bring so much progress that nobody will ever have to pay for pornography, thus putting out of business everybody's favorite pornographer.

I don't know what this world is coming to.

But I have a feeling I'm going to find out.

THE UNOFFICIAL
WEDDING PARTY

FRANCESCA

As wedding season throws its final handful of rice, I've reflected on what it means to be a great wedding guest. Anyone can show up on time, dressed appropriately, with a warm heart and well-wishes for the happy couple. But how can you take your guesthood to the next level? I've identified some key players at every successful wedding. See where you fit in, and make your next RSVP essential.

Up first is the Master of Ceremonies. He or she is that friend with the right mix of warmth and seriousness to pull off the most important duties at the ceremony, like giving a reading or officiating. My buddy has been asked to give a reading at nearly every wedding he's invited to. He's a pop-culture junkie with an English PhD, so he finds the perfect excerpt, whether from an Edith Wharton novel or an episode of *Gilmore Girls.* It's a gift. Don't waste this friend as a ring bearer; a cute dog can do that. Get the Master of Ceremonies front and center to make us all look more mature and responsible than we really are.

Another classic is the Cry Baby. Every wedding needs that one guest to provide the waterworks. I confess, I suck at this. When I was a bridesmaid, I warned my bride that the performance pressure of a wedding blocks my tear ducts like the Hoover Dam. But that's why this role is important, not everyone can do it. Bonus points if you're a male Cry Baby — man-tears catch like wildfire. Daily Double if the Cry Baby is somebody's dad. Don't be embarrassed, a wedding calls for sentimentality, so bring us on home.

I've recently developed a specialty as the Off-the-Cuff Speaker. Speeches are high stakes at a wedding. I'm comfortable with public speaking, and I have a great memory for funny yet flattering anecdotes. As a writer, I can edit on the fly, so that hilarious spring-break story can be rendered appropriate for all audiences. Every newlywed needs that backup speaker in the wings in case the Best Man whiffs it. A good Off-the-Cuff friend ensures the reception is only a glass clink away from rescue.

Once the reception gets rolling, the Crazy

303

Dancer comes in. The Crazy Dancer can be crazy-good, or better yet, just crazy. He or she breaks the seal on looking cool on the dance floor and gives us all permission to cut loose. His manic enthusiasm is contagious and fun, in small doses. Stand near him too long, and you risk being struck by a flailing arm or the tail end of "the worm."

Then there's the Child Star. This kid displays the attention-seeking behavior that can make for a terror in the grocery store but a superstar at a wedding reception. Slick moves in a tiny package, this kid charms everyone by dominating the dance floor — and giving us old people a much-needed breather — until the sugar buzz wears off. With that uninhibited charisma, the Child Star could grow into the next Jimmy Fallon or Jennifer Lawrence . . . or the next Crazy Dancer.

The Social Media Maven. These days, your wedding is part of your personal brand. You need a professional, or a pal who acts like one. The Social Media Maven comes up with a punny hashtag based on the couple's names and posts gorgeous candids of the day online — filtered to perfection, of course. Who can wait two months for professional photos to come out? Newlyweds need bragging rights on Facebook *now*.

Consider yourself #blessed to have a friend like this.

The After-Party Promoter. This person intuits the exact moment when the reception is dying down. Or if intuition isn't your thing, just have the DJ play Bon Jovi's "Livin' on a Prayer" and achieve the same end. The After-Party Promoter somehow knows a solid dive bar in whatever city he's in. He's the patron saint of Patrón. He gets everyone else drunk on shots, yet stays sober enough himself to herd us all back on the party bus or other safe transportation home. At the end of the night, he's the bro-hero you need.

Hopefully you recognized yourself in one of these key roles. But if not, don't worry. You have until next wedding season to hone your skills.

My Brain Hurts
LISA

Have you ever heard the expression, Fool me once, shame on you. Fool me twice, shame on me?

Well, shame on me.

With the plot twist that the person fooling me is myself.

In other words, I'm trying to figure out how and why I make the same mistake twice, over and over.

No, I'm not talking about my marital history.

Thing One and Thing Two were distinctly different mistakes.

I'm talking about dumb little mistakes that I seem to repeat, and for an example, I just did one of them. I was working, and my computer sent me a notice that my keyboard was running out of batteries.

What's the first thing I did?

I ignored it.

That's a dumb thing I do over and over,

but that's not even the dumb thing I'm talking about, which came next.

After a few days, I gave in and changed the batteries, which meant I went downstairs, got the new batteries, brought them upstairs, and shook the old ones out of the computer keyboard.

Then I looked down at the four batteries rolling around my desk.

And I forgot which were the new batteries and which were the old ones.

Of course, I tried sliding any two of them back in the chamber of the keyboard, using as many different combinations I had patience for, but in the end, to no avail.

I had to throw all four batteries away and start over again.

The second time I got it right, but it's a mistake I make every time I have to change batteries, whether it's on the computer mouse, the TV remote controls, or the flashlights. I use twice the number of batteries every year because I have to throw half away.

I know, the solution is simple: just throw the old batteries away first, or at least note the new batteries when you take them out of the package, but I never remember.

And still, none of my flashlights work.

Because flashlights never work.

You know it's true.

And I can't bring myself to change the batteries in my flashlights routinely, because it seems so wasteful of batteries, especially since I have to keep extra on hand to throw away.

And while we're on the subject, I can never remember which way the batteries go in my keyboard. I know that one end of the battery has the thing that sticks out, the alleged "nipple," which is what Thing Two used to call it.

No comment.

And the other end of the battery has the dimple, the little recessed thing that is supposed to fit against the metal contact.

Or whatever.

You see the problem I'm having. I can't describe it because I don't understand it, at all.

I think one side is negative and one is positive, but I don't know which is which.

In any event, when I'm confronted with changing the batteries in my computer keyboard, I have no idea which way they go in.

Like just now, after I had gotten a whole new set of new batteries, it took me fifteen minutes to figure out which way they went in. I had to keep testing the keyboard until

I hit the final combination.

You need a safecracker to get into my keyboard.

And the same thing happened to me yesterday with the remote control. My TV remotes have a back that slides off and each one takes two batteries. At least Comcast gives me a little drawing to help me understand which way the battery goes in, but the diagram was worn away on my older remote and I couldn't read it. So then I tried to reason it out, trying to figure out whether the nipple would go on the spring part or the metal-contact part.

I chose wrongly at first, going for the spring part.

Don't ask me why, it made sense at the time.

If you ever go to a casino, leave me behind.

I did that to both batteries, but they didn't fit in easy, so I had to jam them down on the spring. It should've tipped me off, but I'm not the kind of woman who gives in easily.

When things don't work, I force them.

Then I tested the remote control on the TV, but it didn't work, so I figured by sheer deductive reasoning that I had screwed up yet again.

I took off the back of the remote, figuring

that I could just pop the batteries out and turn them the other way, but I had worked so hard in jamming them on the spring that both batteries were stuck inside the remote and I couldn't get them out.

Impressed yet?

I had to get a butter knife and wedge it under one of the batteries to get them out, which is a time-honored way of dealing with mechanical problems.

Try to follow along, if you're not as talented in the engineering department as I am.

After about twenty minutes, I succeeded in getting the batteries out of the remote, but the metal springs were bent beyond recognition.

I tried to press them down with my finger and mold them into their tiny springy coil, but no luck.

I had to throw away the remote.

So what have we learned?

My brain doesn't work, all the time.

And that batteries are out to get me.

MOTHER TIME
LISA

Tempus fugit.

That's the Latin for, when the hell did *that* happen?

Or, literally, time flies.

I say that because that's how time feels, especially as we get older and we're moving more slowly.

In fact, not only is time flying, but so is everything else, and especially nowadays, when email is the new snail mail.

I can't remember the last handwritten letter I got, but then again, I can't remember anything.

These days, texting seems to be the preferred mode of communication, and it used to be that I texted only with Daughter Francesca and Besties Laura and Franca, but now my plumber will text me and so will any assorted tradespersons, including the guy who came to pick up the PortaJohns after my book club party.

311

And no, his name is not John.

But I digress, because my point is that time is a relative thing, which I think some smart guy said even before me, and I never realized it so much as I did this weekend, and actually, at the book club party.

First some background.

You may know that Francesca and I host a book club party at my house for book clubs who read my April books, to show them our gratitude. We had several hundred people to the house last weekend, on both Saturday and Sunday.

I know it sounds crazy, but Mother Mary told me that if you really want to show someone you care about them, you have to have them over and feed them.

So we do.

And by the way, thanks to you, dear readers. More and more of you are supporting these books because last summer, the most recent in the series, *Does This Beach Make Me Look Fat?* became a *New York Times* bestseller.

Yay!

So thanks are most definitely in order.

Anyway, back to the book club party. We fed them and gave them a show, at which both Francesca and I spoke, telling stories about our writing lives, our dogs, and mostly, each other. And when it was Francesca's turn to speak, she told a funny story about me and happened to say that it drives her crazy when I tell people that she's thirty, because she is only twenty-nine.

That's just the kind of line that made the twenty-somethings in the audience nod in complete understanding.

And the fifty-somethings in the audience laugh and laugh.

Time truly is relative, especially among relatives.

But truly, I never gave validity to this point of hers until I saw all the younger people in our audience nodding, and most of them came up to Francesca later and told her that their mothers did the same thing about their ages and it drove them all crazy, too.

Which is when I started thinking about why we mothers do this, and why it drives our daughters crazy.

And I realized that, for mothers, time is related to memory.

Mother Time.

And I can clearly remember Francesca as an adorable little toddler, all blue eyes and curly blond hair, clutching a yellow giraffe that was her favorite toy. When any adult asked her how old she was, she would hold up three little fingers and say:

"I am this many."

I'm willing to bet that there is no mother reading this who doesn't remember her child saying, "I am this many."

And when you can remember a child saying I-am-this-many, you will have an impossibly difficult time dealing with your child's age at all, once it gets over twelve.

Much less when she starts driving.

Or moves to New York City.

I still can't believe that Francesca is twenty-nine, so, in my mind, it doesn't matter if I round it up to thirty or down to twenty-eight, I feel like all the years blur into one big year, so that a year or two doesn't matter, either way.

Except maybe it does.

Who wouldn't want an extra year at the very end?

So maybe our daughters are trying to teach us something.

Now all I need is sixty fingers.

GOD GAVE YOU TWO

FRANCESCA

I woke up from a dead sleep in the middle of the night to searing pain in my eye, knowing with total certainty that a dog had walked on my face and accidentally scratched my cornea. My first thought?

Not again!

That's right, *again.*

I'm embarrassed to admit that this freak accident has happened to me twice. What are the odds?

Apparently pretty good if you sleep with dogs.

The first injury happened three years ago when I was staying at my mom's house in preparation for our annual book club party. The night before, all five of our Cavalier King Charles spaniels slept with me — I'm their favorite — and as I was waking up, one of my mom's puppies got excited to say good morning. He snuggled and squirmed all over my face, and, in a badly timed blink, he caught my eyeball with one of his claws.

I knew it was bad, because I could feel the flap of my torn cornea when I blinked.

Hope you aren't squeamish.

I went to the ER and came back in time to co-host the party, I'm hard-core like that, but by the end of the day, my eye had swollen shut like a prizefighter's.

They say the cornea of the eye has more nerve endings than any other part of the body. I felt all of them.

I lay in bed trembling for the next few days, and that was with prescription pain medication. My eye did not reopen for two weeks, and full vision didn't return for over a month. I still have complications from it.

I remember my ophthalmologist asking, "Does the dog *have* to sleep in the bed with you?"

Um, yes?

And exactly three years later, home at my mom's for the book club party, sleeping in a bed with five dogs, one scratched my eye again.

The good news: this scratch wasn't as bad as the last one, and I'll make a full recovery. And in this case, it happened the day *after* the book club party. And finally, it happened to my *other* eye.

That last one is arguably good news, since

this was supposed to be my *good* eye, but hey, God gave you two for a reason.

You're thinking, surely now I'll stop sleeping with dogs in the bed, right?

Ah, no.

What is wrong with me? Am I stubborn or stupid?

Probably both.

But dogs-in-the-bed is a way of life. As a little girl, I shared my bed with up to three golden retrievers. I told them stories before I fell asleep. Their snores were my lullabies. Their fluffy bellies were my big spoon.

My current dog, Pip, has slept in my bed since he was a puppy. Cuddling him is an essential part of my routine to unwind. And every morning, instead of reaching for my cell phone and scrolling through emails first thing, I roll over and reach for his fluffy little body.

Caffeine for the soul.

Ironically, I'm not much of a cuddler when it comes to sleeping with humans. When past boyfriends have gallantly invited me to lay my head on their shoulder, I invariably get pins and needles in my ear. And I know it's cute when girls complain of being cold all the time (we get it, you're skinny), but I run hot. I get overheated sleeping against another body, and it's not fun for anyone. An ex called me his "little furnace."

A dog, on the other hand, takes up less space, doesn't have to get up for work before you, and only farts *above* the covers.

And to get serious for a minute, my dog was crucial to my emotional recovery after being assaulted. I struggled the most at night; when I would close my eyes to go to sleep, my mind obsessively replayed the attack. But placing a hand on Pip, burying my fingers in his soft coat, and listening to his little snorts were the only things that broke that cycle. His tactile presence pulled me back to the safety of the moment and filled me with a sense of comfort and love.

So the dog stays.

My eyes will just have to be more careful going forward.

And look, the ophthalmologist also said that cats are typically the pets that cause eye injuries. So I told the cat she is not allowed on my bed.

She just jumps up anyway.

(I'd wink, but I already am.)

In the Soup
LISA

Once upon a time, I had the great idea that I was going to try to make butternut-squash soup.

And as soon as I started, I realized almost immediately that this was a terrible idea.

By way of background, I got the idea because I had just come back from a book tour, so I was meeting a lot of wonderful, brilliant, beautiful people, by which I mean, people who read my books.

Yes, you.

I love you.

I'm grateful to my readers because I feel so blessed and/or lucky to be able to make a living telling stories, whether fictional or all too real, like the ones contained in this book. And because I feel so grateful to my readers, I love to go on book tour and actually meet them, and my book signings are not typical, to say the least.

I don't read my own book aloud at my

book signings because my readers are fully capable of doing that all by themselves. Instead I tell them the story of what inspired the book, how I got to be a writer, or funny family stories, and the conversation opens up pretty quickly into questions, which begin with readers asking me about my creative process and end with us gabbing about life, love, dogs, and carbohydrates.

We even exchange recipes.

It's not a cookbook signing, it's a girl signing, which is basically the same thing.

This is even more true when Francesca and I tour for these books, because we put on a little mother-and-daughter show which entertains our readers, and we all end up hugging, fighting, or weeping.

Which is basically the same thing, too.

It's an estrogenfest.

Or an estrogen-replacement fest.

Bottom line, it's fun.

So it was during one of my signings that one of my readers started telling me about all the wonderful soups she made for autumn; and then the conversation segued into Crock-Pots and soup recipes, and you can see how this led to the butternut-squash recipe in question.

Which begins with butternut squash.

And should end right there.

By the way, I have never ever owned a Crock-Pot, though Mother Mary did, and I ordered one up right away, excited. It's just my kind of toy because it came with no directions, except plug it in and don't burn down the house.

Gotcha.

I had a butternut-squash recipe in mind because my reader told me that all I had to do was get a butternut squash, peel it, chop it up, roast it with olive oil, and throw it in the Crock-Pot with water and voilà.

But I was stumped at the threshold.

First off, thank God for the signs in the produce section, because my grocery store has a positively bewildering array of squash, most of which is decorative.

I didn't make that mistake.

I'm not cooking the centerpiece.

Before I saw the squash signs, I had no idea which squash was the butternut and I became dazed scanning the squash varieties, all of which are shaped like a blunt object, color-coordinated to autumn.

Finally I found the butternut squash, which looked nothing like butter, nuts, or whatever a butternut is. Next to the butternut squash was a special bin that showed butternut squash already chopped and covered in plastic.

That should've tipped me off, right there.

But no, I was a butternut-squash virgin and didn't recognize the red flag, produce-wise.

I bypassed the precut squash in favor of the real experience.

Accept no substitutes.

I hoisted the biggest of the butternut squash, which qualified as working out, and sat it down in the front compartment of my cart, showing it off like the small child that it resembled.

Also it was visible proof that I was buying an actual food thing, marking me as a true home cook.

Then I brought it home and gave it a bath.

I should've put it to bed, because at this point, it was ten o'clock since I hadn't had any time to food shop that day. But no worries, I figured that it would take maybe an hour at most to make the soup, since that's what I had remembered my reader telling me.

So I located a peeler and set to work.

Already it was annoying.

My peeler is ancient, and it rattled away as I managed to scrape off the weird outer skin of the butternut squash, apparently made of plastic. The shape of the thing — I don't know whether it's a fruit, a vegetable, or a lethal instrument — was almost impossible to peel evenly, but I persevered, feeling vaguely colonial.

I was connecting to all of the women through time who dug up the earth, scraped off vegetables with sharp rocks, then boiled them in cauldrons over fires, like witches with better clothes.

But peeling was only the first hurdle, because then there was chopping.

I grabbed a utility knife that I use all the time and tried to cut the squash, but the blade would only go through a quarter of the way. I moved it down off the non-bulbous portion of the squash, but that was equally dense, and as hard as I pressed, it wouldn't work.

I dug in the drawer for another knife and tried it, but its blade was too thin and got stuck.

I went back to the drawer and tried my last good knife, which was a paring knife, but it was too short and cut only a wedge.

By now, I'm sweating.

So I'm cutting and sweating, and sweating and cutting, then swearing and mangling the butternut squash with my tiny paring knife.

And I'm wishing I'd bought the precut slices.

Because instead of the neat one-inch slices that my reader told me to make, I'm excising chunks from the body of the butternut squash, like Shylock getting his pound of flesh.

It wasn't pretty.

And it took forever.

I wasn't ready to start roasting the chunks until eleven thirty and I'd remembered my reader telling me they have to roast for an hour, so at twelve fifteen at night, I was standing drowsily in front of my oven, praying for sleep.

So of course I take the squash chunks out of the oven before they're completely cooked and try to purée them, which only jams up the Vita-whatever, but I persevered, and even though I'd made a chunky mess, I dumped it in the ceramic part of the Crock-Pot and stuck it in the refrigerator to cook it tomorrow.

Which is today.

Even if it tastes good, I'll never do it again.

What a crock.

LOOK OUT! THERE'S A FEMINIST BEHIND YOU.

FRANCESCA

As Halloween approaches, scares pop up everywhere: haunted houses, spooky decorations, horror movies. The scariest word?

Feminist.

Boo!

Are you terrified? Was Meryl Streep? When asked in a recent interview if she considered herself a feminist, Streep answered:

"I'm a humanist."

My head spun like Linda Blair's in *The Exorcist.*

I barely flinch at the nervous equivocating or outright rejection of feminism coming from young starlets. I chalk that up to the ignorance of youth or the real fear of alienating the powerful men who remain the gatekeepers in Hollywood.

But my beloved Meryl? Sixty-six years old, nineteen Oscar nominations, and three wins deep, and *she's* afraid of "feminist"?

To use horror-movie jargon, I thought Meryl was our *final girl.* The one who escaped the career-axing patriarchy and survived to tell the tale.

If we lose her, there's no hope for a sequel.

I understand Meryl was trying to say she believes in the equality of all humans (which, for what it's worth, isn't what "humanist" means), but our society does not currently offer equality between the sexes, so if you're for equality between men and women, then you are a . . .

Feminist.

I'm going to keep saying it until we all get comfortable with the word. Exposure therapy is the best way to treat phobias.

And I'm not suggesting Meryl is a sexist, she's not. Later in the Q&A, she articulated several pointed examples of the way Hollywood needs to change to achieve equality for women.

Yet she wouldn't say the word.

I also get that she's trying to sell a movie, and it's imperative that she avoid scaring off ticket buyers. But the irony here is the film is *Suffragette.*

Somewhere, Susan B. Anthony's zombie hand just shot up from her grave.

Does it matter if someone accepts the word "feminist" if her actions and opinions

326

support the cause?

Yes.

Words matter.

Imagine you are a child, and you watch adult women shudder and sidestep the word, or you see men roll their eyes at it, what do you learn?

Feminists are bad. Feminists are annoying. Feminists are unwanted. Feminists are scary.

Perpetuating the fear around the word "feminist" perpetuates sexism.

We fear what we don't understand, so let's review an accurate definition for the word:

A feminist is a person who believes that men and women should have equal rights and opportunities.

It doesn't mean a person who hates men (that's a misandrist), nor does it mean you think men and women are exactly the same in all ways. It definitely doesn't mean any of the boogey-women that misogynists like to whisper about across a campfire:

"I held the door for one of those feminazis, and she cried, 'RAPE!' "

"I asked a feminist out on a date, and when she said 'no, thanks,' I saw that she HAS NEVER SHAVED."

These are urban legends for idiots.

And yet the more subtle myths have

seeped into the mainstream. For example, women, do you fear that if you call yourself a feminist, boys won't like you anymore?

The ones who won't weren't the ones you'd want anyway.

Men, do you fear that if she calls herself a feminist, she won't need you anymore?

Equal pay will buy sheets with a higher thread count, but it doesn't keep us warm at night.

If you're afraid of a feminist, you've been duped by those who wish to maintain the sexist status quo. The bad juju surrounding the word is all just spooky violin music and jump cuts that the patriarchy adds in post-production.

Look there at that female CEO, she's not a "dragon lady," you can see the boom mic in the corner of the frame.

That girl with "resting bitch face"? She's not being nasty, she's just not flirting with the male character beside her.

A feminist might be your hardworking mother or your well-brought-up son. We're reasonable people supporting a more-than-reasonable cause, with nary a ski mask in sight.

So I dare you to go into the bathroom at midnight and say "Bloody Mary" three times, and then look in the mirror — a

feminist will appear!
  You.

MUTED

LISA

There's an old Italian proverb that says, great griefs are mute.

I believe that because I live it.

I lost my father Frank Scottoline to blood cancer on December 10, 2002. He lived his life as a peaceful, easy-going man, and he passed away the same way. His life, and his death, were in many ways the polar opposite of my feisty Mother Mary, such a force of nature that once I began to write about her, she got all the headlines.

But that doesn't mean my father didn't matter, or that his loss wasn't felt.

I don't know if you've had this experience yourself, but grief is the gift that keeps on taking.

You think you're over it, whatever that means, but grief crops up from time to time, triggered by a memory or thought, an article of clothing, or even a song.

For me, it's a time of year.

Autumn.

My father's illness was chronic CLL, which is a form of blood cancer that isn't life-threatening unless it morphs into its most aggressive mutation, called Richter's Syndrome. Though the odds of the Richter's mutation are very low, that was exactly what happened to my father, and by summer, he was fighting for his life, and by Thanksgiving we worried we were going to lose him.

He didn't live until Christmas.

Though I had already bought presents for him, a child's wish unfulfilled.

He passed away in the hospital, with my stepmother Fayne and me by his side, only an hour after my brother Frank had arrived. It was a predictably horrible scene, and I've written about it in previous books, but I'm making a different point herein.

Because now, almost thirteen years later, as the days get shorter and darker and the air begins to chill to the bone, my heart knows before my brain does that it's the time of year that my father died.

There's no fooling the memory of the human heart.

And so today, on Veterans Day, I found myself online, trying to find his military records because he was in a branch of the armed services that existed then, the Army

331

Air Force, as a radio operator. I couldn't find his records because I had the inevitable tussle with ancestry.com and other sites to sign in, remember my password, and all that fol-de-rol, which put me off. But the search turned up his death notice, which is so remarkable that it took me back to the days following his passing, and I felt again the sorrow, confusion, and oddly inappropriate humor of that time.

If you have ever written a death notice, planned a funeral, or tried to think when your world is crashing down around you, I'm hoping you can relate to the following story.

We were at my house, having just picked out my father's casket. My stepmother was over my house, slumped in my living-room chair, heartbroken. Francesca was only in high school then, so she was home but she was upstairs. My brother Frank was also there, but he was in the kitchen with my husband at the time.

My second ex-husband.

Or, Thing Two.

Only two days later, I would ask Thing Two to leave the house for good, immediately after my father's funeral, but we didn't know that then.

That's another story.

I know, right? I have a dramatic life.

Don't we all?

In any event, I was at home and I got a telephone call from *The Philadelphia Inquirer,* which is our local newspaper, asking me if I wanted to put in a death notice. I told them yes, and I figured I would handle it to give my stepmother a break, so I began to dictate what the death notice should say.

As you may know, if you have read either my fiction or previous volumes in this series, I have a half-sister that I didn't meet until I was an adult, who was my father's daughter, born outside his marriage to my mother. Her name is Jeanne, and she was put up for adoption and lived a very happy life with her adoptive family, but decided to find her birth father when she was an adult, and we all got to know one another, after we got over the initial shock.

I was shocked, my father wasn't.

Neither was my stepmother. Or Mother Mary.

Dramatic, right?

Jeanne was going to come to Philadelphia for my father's funeral, and when it came time to compose a death notice, I wanted to make sure she was included. My father had a wonderful relationship with her, and so had my stepmother, and I wanted Jeanne to know she was part of the family.

So my intent was pure, but my execution horrible.

I described to the woman from the newspaper all of the relatives that needed to be named in the death notice — the children, the stepchildren, and when we came to Jeanne, I wasn't quite sure what to call her. I figured that she was my half-sister, so that would make her my father's half-daughter, and that's what I told the woman on the phone.

"What did you say?" the woman asked, her tone surprised.

"I said she's my half-sister, so she's his half-daughter. Please make sure you include her."

"Are you sure?" The woman still sounded surprised, which I chalked up to the fact that I was including my heretofore-unknown half-sister in the death notice.

"I'm absolutely sure," I told her, then I launched into the story, because I can tell a story on autopilot, especially when I am exhausted, sad, happy, or all of the above.

I wake up emotional.

I finished the story by saying, ". . . and so she came to look for her birth father, and she found him, and that was my father, so I would like you to include her in the notice as his half-daughter."

"Okay, if that's the way you want it."

"Yes, that's exactly the way I want it. Thank you."

I hung up feeling good about myself, and just then Francesca came into the room.

"Mom," she said, frowning, "what did you just say to that lady on the phone?"

"I told her that I wanted to include Jeanne in the death notice because she deserves to be acknowledged and welcomed into this family."

Again, proud of myself. Demonstrating to growing daughter that there was a way to rise above family secrets and do the right thing.

Francesca was still frowning. "But you know there's no such thing as a half-daughter, right?"

"What?" My head hurt. I had no idea what Jeanne was to Francesca, who, like me, had found out that she had an aunt later than usual. "Jeanne is my half-sister, so she's my father's half-daughter."

"No, she's not." Francesca looked at me like I was crazy. "She's his full daughter. She's his *daughter.* Like you."

I gasped. "Oh my God. Really?"

"There is no such thing as a half-daughter. I'm in AP Bio."

Suddenly it struck me that Francesca was right. She was in AP Bio and I was grief-stricken but didn't know it. My brain simply wasn't working.

I scrambled to call the newspaper back, but I couldn't get the same woman on the phone, and I couldn't get the notice corrected. It ran in the paper just as I had dictated it, saying that my father is "survived by his half daughter Jeanne . . ."

They didn't have a hyphen between half and daughter.

It should have been *half-daughter.*

More appropriate to a word that didn't exist.

Arg.

Of course when I saw Jeanne, I explained what had happened with the death notice and apologized profusely. She laughed it off in her peaceful, easy-going way.

Which she got from my father.

And that was the exact notice that I found today on Veterans Day, when I went online, trying to find my father's military records.

Because I realize now that I wasn't looking for his military records at all.

I was looking for him.

Pieces of him that got left behind, that showed up online somewhere.

Something, anything.

But all I found was a memory.
And a story, happy and sad, both at once.
I wanted to tell it to you.
And now it will remain.
Mute.

AARP, or American Association of Retired Pets
LISA

It's no secret that I'm getting older, and so are my pets.

But only one of us is able to retire, and it ain't me.

I've always had dogs and cats, as well as the usual menagerie of pets that populated Francesca's childhood, like guinea pigs, a gerbil, and even a pygmy bunny named Peewee, who lived to be twelve years old.

Peewee was a sweet gray rabbit, who loved to be cuddled, and Francesca made sure of same, by cuddling him at every opportunity. He had soft gray eyes, a pinkish nose that moved almost constantly, and a heart-shaped mouth, which would've been adorable except for the fact that he had one tooth that actually grew outside of his mouth and up his nose.

Yes, that happened.

Twice.

Luckily, my vet had seen this before and

was able to snip the tooth both times, and though it grew back, at least Peewee got some oxygen.

It's tough to breathe with a tooth up your nose.

This background is by way of saying that I'm familiar with pets and how wonderful they are, how much they can love you, and how much you can love them in return, as well as the sad fact that they pass away. I have had all of our pets cremated, and their remains are in my office as we speak, stored in little cedar chests with a sympathy card from the vet.

Shout-out to all the vets who do thoughtful things like writing a sympathy card to pet owners when their pets pass away.

Your kindness does not go unnoticed, believe me.

My point is that I know pets die, but what is coming as a surprise as I've gotten older is that my pets are aging along with me, and something else is happening at this point. By that I mean, in the past I always felt that my age was a constant, and I was in temporal standstill, while my pets got older and passed away.

But that is no longer the case.

This revelation dawned on me only slowly, because that's the way I am, when I realized that my back was a little achy in the morning. It happened because I'd been on deadline, so I'd been sitting a lot at the computer, and of course the first thing that gets jettisoned when there's work to be done is exercise.

In contrast, there's always time for meals.

It's a bad combination.

In any event, I got out of the chair yesterday, feeling sluggish and unsteady, and I stumbled just a little. At the same moment, I just happened to look over at Little Tony, who had gotten out of the chair because I did, and he stumbled a little before he stood up.

The comparison was undeniable, though only one of us has fur.

(Me, on my legs.)

And then I thought about the relative ages of the pets, realizing that Tony, whom I still thought of as a new dog, was about seven years old, and that Ruby is even older. I got her when Francesca went to college, as a daughter replacement.

It almost worked.

But only because Ruby is a corgi, a breed that is just as much fun, and just as much trouble, as a daughter.

I calculated quickly and realized that Ruby is almost thirteen years old, and obviously infirm. As I've written before, she has developed degenerative myelopathy, which means that her back legs are paralyzed and she has to use a little wheeled cart to walk.

Still she gets around better than I do. I had some ramps built at the front and back doors, and she shoots down them like she's at NASCAR. In fact, she speeds everywhere around the house, catching her wheels' legs on the table and the corners of the walls, but she crashes ahead willy-nilly and yesterday, she ran over Tony.

Ruby is a bad driver, even for a dog.

The most touching thing is that she still can walk, in her dreams.

When she falls asleep on the rug, there will inevitably be a time when all of her forelegs start to wiggle in a way they can't when she's awake. At first I thought it was seizures, but it's more regular, clearly her legs in a walking and running motion, obeying whatever nerves still exist.

We can always dream, can't we?

Even corgis.

But she still needs special care, and I have to take her out of her cart and lift her upstairs, or onto the bed, or outside to go to the bathroom.

Every time I pick her up to carry her somewhere, she squirms and looks down,

Nothing stops Ruby.

trying to right herself. She'll even bark and growl at the other dogs as they run around us, barking up at her. She used to be the leader of the pack, but her grip on power is loosening, and they sense it. They know she's on the decline, and so does she. They're already angling for position, in their minds.

The Queen is dead, long live the Queen.

Ruby weighs thirty-five pounds, and I confess to you that in the old days, I might've complained about having to lug her everywhere.

But I don't feel that way anymore.

Ruby runs her cart into a ditch. Boone and Tony attempt to change a tire.

I feel more tender with her than I ever have.

I *get* her, now.

She's feisty, funny, smart, and accustomed to doing everything for herself as well as running the house.

Sound familiar?

And she still feels that way inside, but her body is undeniably aging.

Check, check, check.

I feel sorry for her that she's no longer the undisputed queen and is sometimes even ignored.

Every middle-aged woman knows what it's like to feel marginalized.

And we don't like it.

The more I perform these little tasks for her, hugging her dense little body close, the more I have come to feel a tender kinship with her.

She needs me, in a way she didn't before.

And I realize how much I need her and value her particular brand of feistiness, which persists despite all common sense.

I know I will cry when Ruby passes.

And I will have her remains cremated and stored in a cedar box behind me, with a sympathy card written by a vet who sees her only twice a year but still understands how I feel to lose her.

Because that loss will come hard.

Maybe even hardest of all.

And now I know why.

They're Playing My Song

FRANCESCA

When I first laid eyes on my ex-boyfriend, he was on a stage. I'd gone with friends to his concert without expectation, but I found myself mesmerized by him, his passionate performance, and his songs full of heartache.

I was a face in a crowd, but I was already thinking I could heal that music.

Like every woman who hears a sad love song.

Only then we actually did.

For the two years we were together, I tried to go to every single gig he played in the city, big or small. I wanted to support him and help out, I hauled my share of equipment and stood in empty parking spots like a human traffic cone while he drove the van around the block, but I also loved watching him perform.

Professional and personal worlds are often kept separate, so I felt lucky to get to see the person I loved doing the thing he loved. And when I could hear traces of us in his music, I felt especially close to him, like no part of his life was wholly apart from me. A rhyme he asked for my input on, or a guitar lick he discovered from the edge of my bed, were precious breadcrumbs that only I could follow. I felt like the special secret keeper in the audience.

Which is not to say I knew all his secrets. Early on, most of the songs he sang in concert predated our relationship, and I actively tried not to think about whom they were about. But I'm only human, and once or twice I caved and asked him if a song was about anyone specific.

He would shrug it off and say, "Not really."

I knew this could be a white lie, but it rang true at the time. He had only a couple love songs, and their angle wasn't particularly flattering to their female subject. We were twenty-five when we met, so it was possible he hadn't had a great love worthy of a great love song.

I had a feeling we were on our way.

I got my wish the next year, when he wrote a classic soul ballad about us. The lyrics were as good as it gets in "my boy-friend's in a band" land. He captured the euphoria of our present and the excitement for our future together. He sent me an early, stripped-down version of him singing it into an iPhone, which I probably played a hundred times.

That WAV file would have been enough for me, but seeing him perform it in person was even better. We had a brass section! Love deserves a brass section.

Sometimes he would introduce the song and point me out in the crowd, making every head in the room turn to stare in envy. I'd avoid their eyes and look at him, unable to suppress a smile of equal parts embarrassment and joy. It used to make my heart race.

I cried the first time I saw him perform it.

I also cried the last time, when it was the end before the end — that wretched, miserable time when you both know a relationship is on its last legs. Knowing the plans in that soaring chorus wouldn't come true gutted me.

And everyone else dancing, looking at me in envy all the same.

I no longer felt like the keeper of secrets in the audience, I felt like the coconspirator of a lie.

I waited almost a year after we broke up before going to see him perform again. I was back on my feet, feeling like myself again, and my ex and I had formed a solid friendship from the rubble — occasional emails, friendly meals, that sort of thing. I had dated other people since him, too. I felt bullet-proof. So when he invited me to the launch of his new album, I said yes.

But standing in that Brooklyn venue, listening to those songs again, watching him onstage, it felt the same in all the ways that didn't matter — the almost-cold beer, the concrete floor, the silhouettes of heads, the blue-and-gold lighting — and different in all the ways that did.

I still watch him perform like a girlfriend, part stage-mom, part-hawk. I still appraise his outfit, and he still wears the chambray shirt I bought him when I set out to upgrade his stage wardrobe. I still lift the corners of my mouth to telepathically keep his pitch up during that one note when he tends to go flat. I still smile when he nails it.

I still think he looks great, and I still have radar for the girls in the audience who agree with me.

But I don't stand front and center like I used to. I tuck myself back left.

Front and center is for eye-sexing, and now we are just eye-friends.

Speaking of sex, some of the old songs

were fun to hear again, like that one song he wrote about me.

Mm-hm, that's right.

The language is veiled, but that's what it's about. How do I know for sure? For one, he told me so when he was writing it.

And two, I recognize my moves.

The song is entitled "Exorcism," which I'm actually proud of.

If you date a musician and *don't* leave him with a song about sex-demon possession, you went too easy on him.

At one point during the song, a tall guy with curly hair dancing near me tapped me on the shoulder and leaned in to say something over the music.

"Your hair smells amazing."

I smiled. It was too dark for him to see me blush.

"You like this band?"

The irony made me laugh. "They're not bad."

I'm not going to lie, there's a certain satisfaction to getting hit on while your ex milks the crowd with a song about you.

But it was too weird, and I felt almost guilty. I excused myself to get a beer.

My ex cannot play the sound track to my next meet-cute.

This will probably not surprise you, but I

don't like the song he wrote about our breakup. He's certainly entitled to his own spin on our parting, but that doesn't mean I have to dig it. Honestly, I could live with the fact that it oversimplifies things — there are only so many bars — but I hate that it reduces us to cliché.

We deserved better metaphors.

Did he forget his ex is a writer?

Though I confess, the chorus — a chorus about being free of me — got stuck in my head. It's very catchy, which is almost rude.

I had heard it before only because he released a video for it online, so at least I listened to it first in private. But while that mental preparation removed some of the lyrics' sting, it was a surreal and unpleasant experience to be surrounded by people dancing to the beat of breaking my heart.

But by far, the hardest part was hearing our happy love ballad back in rotation. I guess I shouldn't have been surprised. And I don't blame him. It's a good song, and it's his product to sell.

But man, he sold it.

How did those words make him feel? Did they take him back like they did me? Or had he detached so much that the lyrics no longer held emotional truth, now they're just words that rhymed?

Maybe they always were.

Perhaps he's gotten used to the distance by now. There's an element of artifice to any performance. He rehearses these songs, plays them again and again, sells them to new people, woos new women with them.

Some other woman will listen to it and think, "I could be that girl." And she'll hear the breakup one and think, "I could heal that."

And if she asks him if it's about anyone specific, he'll answer, "Not really."

And maybe, by then, it will be true.

But it will never be true for me. Few things are as evocative of memory as music. Songs are emotions preserved in sap. Those are my emotions, so those are my songs.

When I went home from the concert that night, I knew then that I wouldn't go to any more of his shows. Because no matter how "over it" I am in real life, it's impossible to listen to him sing the words to real feelings we felt and not have my chest in knots. Watching him *perform* them only makes me feel more freakishly vulnerable by comparison.

He's the one up onstage, with the microphone, and the brass backup, and the applause at the end.

And I'm a face in the crowd, imagining I know what he means.

To Error Is Human

LISA

There's a lesson in every news story.

Luckily, you have me to find it for you.

Today's news story is the driverless car, about which you might have heard.

It's an Audi SUV outfitted with special electronics by a company named Delphi Automotive, and those electronics enable the car to drive itself. In fact, the car left San Francisco last weekend and is now driving itself thirty-five hundred miles to New York City.

I'm not making this up. I saw it online, so you know it's real.

The car is due to arrive in New York this weekend.

It better be on time.

And it probably will be.

Why?

Because there's no people around to make it late.

In fact, that's the theory of the driverless

car. That it can drive itself anywhere, speed up or slow down, switch lanes, enter and exit highways, merge, and in short, get itself where it wants to even safer than a "human-piloted" car.

Why?

Because to err is human, and if you want to eliminate the err, you have to eliminate the human.

In other words, there's no pilot to mess up the piloting.

No knucklehead's at the wheel to text, eat, talk on the phone, or swill vodka while driving, nobody to be distracted or sleepy, no man or woman to make the mistakes that humans inevitably make.

And don't get me started on teenagers, who, though adorable, are programmed to make more driving mistakes than the general population.

It's not their fault, it's their hormones.

In that they have them.

There are few fuels more powerful than high-octane testosterone.

And at certain times of the month, estrogen can light an entire city.

I barely remember my estrogen.

And I'm not trying to replace her.

Because I don't miss her.

Nor does anyone around me.

When you think about it, the idea of a driverless car is very simple, and in fact, I wonder why it took so long to accomplish.

After all, planes have autopilot, so why shouldn't cars?

I know what you're thinking, that there's a lot more things to bump into on the road than in the sky, but you're forgetting that there's one big thing you could bump into in the sky, which is that large round ball located beneath the plane.

If you hit it, you'll do more than bend your fender.

The downside risk is greater. As in, it's *down.*

You get the idea, even if Harrison Ford doesn't.

So how does the driverless car get where it wants to go?

The Delphi website says that the car has "four short-range radars, three vision-based cameras, six lidars, a localization system, intelligent software algorithms and a full suite of Advanced Driver Assistance Systems."

Cheater.

If I had all that stuff, I could drive myself around, too.

Oh. Wait.

Plus I don't know what a lidar is, and I

don't care. I don't need any lidars to drive my car. All I need is a fresh cup of coffee, my phone, something to eat, and a dead mouse in a water bottle.

You may recall the time I was driving, drank a dead mouse, and almost crashed into a divider, a cyclone fence, and a Wawa store.

Because I'm a human being.

And therefore unworthy of being a pilot.

I'm loving this principle of eliminating humans to reduce error, and I'm wondering if we could apply it in other situations.

For example, I'm pretty sure that both of my marriages would have been an astounding success, if I hadn't been in either one of them.

Also, I think the country would be running better if we eliminated the human beings in government.

Oh wait. There aren't any.

What if we just took the human beings off the planet and let Earth run itself?

Let's see, the air would smell better, the water would run cleaner, the ground would remain unpunctured, and the animals would be safe.

Just the way we found it.

Before we started driving.

Nah.

CONDITIONAL
LISA

Every woman has a hair history.

Or is it a hairstory?

Let me tell you mine, then I'll get to my point.

We began, as always, with The Flying Scottolines, and growing up, we all used the same bathroom, which contained exactly one bottle of shampoo.

Head & Shoulders.

By the way, none of us had dandruff.

Those white spots on our clothes were lint.

I can't explain why Mother Mary always bought us Head & Shoulders, except that I suspect she thought it was fancier than our old shampoo, which was called Suave.

By the way, we weren't suave, either.

We aspired to being suave, with dandruff.

I come from a long line of aspirational shampoo buyers.

In any event, we used our creamy aqua Head & Shoulders shampoo and felt pretty good about ourselves, until one day, when I was in high school. I was with my first boyfriend at a party, which was held outside. It was August, which is definitely a bad-hair month in Philly.

Which is a bad-hair city.

You know it's true.

It's the City of Brotherly Locks.

For women.

Anyway, back to the party. My curly, frizzy, wavy hair had already exploded, and my boyfriend made the mistake of trying to touch my hair.

This was back in the old days, when men actually touched my hair.

Overrated.

Anyway, his hand got caught in my hair and he couldn't get it out, as if I had the Venus flytrap of hair.

I caught a man!

Then I tore off his wings.

Just kidding.

In fact, I was completely embarrassed, and after my boyfriend finally freed his fingers from my carnivorous hair, he said, "You should really use a conditioner."

I didn't even know what conditioner was. And that's how naïve I was, back then. I was a conditioner virgin.

So I went home and told Mother Mary

that we needed conditioner, and after much grumbling, on her next trip to the grocery store, she returned home with something that purported to be shampoo and conditioner in the same bottle, called Pert Plus.

Like I said, aspirational.

I may not be suave, but I'm nothing if not Pert Plus.

So I used the stuff, but the truth is, it didn't seem to make any difference. My hair was still tangly, curly, wavy, and frizzy, and on occasion, my own hand got stuck in it.

Medusa, needing mousse.

So I consulted my girlfriends and all of them agreed that the two-in-one products didn't work and that I needed conditioner that came in its own bottle, so I went to ask my mother.

"No," Mother Mary said flatly. "We don't need two bottles in the shower."

"But it will change my life," I argued, meaning it.

"No it won't. It won't even change your hair."

Mother Mary ruled the house, so fast-forward to the present day, when I get my own house, with a shower all to myself.

It's filled with approximately twelve different bottles of conditioner.

No two-in-ones for this girl.

Each one separate from shampoo.

Head and shoulders above everything else.

Very suave.

And every time I wash my hair, I use conditioner in the shower, then I spray on a detangler and comb through with Moroccan oil.

The result?

My hair looks greasy all the time.

There is so much damn product in my hair that even the smallest dollop of shampoo explodes on contact with my head, which is the telltale sign of product overload.

Also I produce so much lather that I'm wearing a meringue pie.

Evidently, each time I shampoo, I'm shampooing the conditioner.

And I don't know how to stop the madness.

So I asked my girlfriends, who told me there's a special shampoo you can buy and a special conditioner you can use, which together will somehow strip out all of the other shampoos and conditioners.

But I'm not buying.

Do I need more product to eliminate my product?

I'm beginning to suspect that Mother

Mary was right, yet again.
She loved me, unconditionally.

DOG MUST LOVE

FRANCESCA

For the twenty-four hours that I had an active Tinder account, my bio consisted of one line:

"I don't introduce my dog to just anyone."

"Must love dogs" is a given. But any man dating me ought to recognize this:

My dog has to love you.

You know how dogs can sense ghosts and smell fear? They have even more experience smelling assholes.

My first boyfriend tried valiantly to be a dog person, but he was asthmatic and allergic to all things furry. That he dated me, the only girl in our high school who had four dogs, a cat, and a horse, was an exercise in masochism.

In gratitude, I pretended not to notice when his nose was runny when we kissed.

Young love.

Despite his allergies, all the dogs adored him, especially our one golden retriever, Angie. She would shuffle over to him and face-plant in his lap.

She got to third base before I did.

He was a patient, gentle, sniffly boy, and an ideal first boyfriend. We dated for years.

My college boyfriend was one of those guys who only knew how to interact with animals by rough-housing with them. When he visited my home in the summer, he completely won over our youngest golden retriever, Penny, by matching her manic energy for jumping into the pool after the ball.

He scored fewer points with my horse, Willie. Within minutes of mounting up for his first-ever riding lesson, my ex considered himself a cowboy. He had enough fear to hold the reins in a death grip, but enough false bravado to deliver a wallop of a kick when I had advised "a squeeze."

Willie started walking backwards, tail switching, ears pinned back. The horse shot me a look with a rolling eye that said: "Let him try that one more time, and see where he lands."

Our first and last lesson ended shortly after that.

And our relationship ended a few months later.

Willie was right. He kept me on too short a rein.

I dated one guy in the city who probably should've been a fling, but he was so enthusiastic about my dog Pip, and Pip so crazy about him, I fell in love. Pip was only a couple years old then, and this guy would always play with him first thing when he came over. Pip adored him, which made me adore him. The fact that my dog liked him seemed to vouch for his trustworthiness.

Until one morning when I got up to see him playing with Pip buck naked, dangling Pip's favorite chew toy dangerously close to other dangly bits.

He was a little too trusting.

Then there was that guy I was so excited about. I thought he was sophisticated, intelligent, successful, a real catch. Until he met Pip.

"Can I pick him up?" he asked.

I found it an endearing request.

I have never in my life seen someone pick up an animal so awkwardly. His approach was totally illogical. He just sort of hugged Pip's neck under one front leg and pulled up, making the dog's ruff smoosh around his face, his arm sticking out like a Popsicle stick, his back feet scrambling in the air.

I swooped in to take my precious baby

from this oaf.

I could feel my ovaries recoil.

Next!

Sometimes I do give second chances. Like my musician-boyfriend — when we first started dating, he made a show of cringing and clutching his ear whenever Pip barked, as if the sound threatened his instrument. I found it so histrionic, I complained to all my girlfriends about it, and I was on the verge of breaking things off with him two weeks in.

But communication is key. So I told him it made me feel terrible every time he did that, and he was touched, mistakenly believing I felt terrible for his annoyance, not *at* it.

A harmless misunderstanding I chose not to correct.

He stopped grousing and grew to love Pip, even with the occasional barking.

And Pip loved him back. He would drag me toward my boyfriend's van or any car that looked like his van whenever we walked down the street. And Pip would give him morning kisses before I could.

I had visions of a future furry family.

But sometimes forces beyond a dog's opinion pull a relationship apart. On the night that we actually broke up — even though there was no fighting, just tears and hugging — somehow, Pip knew.

After we had said our last good-byes at the door to my apartment, my ex said, "Wait, I want to say good-bye to Pip."

I knew this scene would rip my heart out, but how could I say no? I agreed and stepped aside. He called his name.

Pip was visible from the entranceway, lying down in front of my bed, watching. He didn't move.

"C'mere, boy." He patted his knee.

Pip did not budge. Not even a tail flutter.

Ice. Cold.

Woman's best friend.

THE GODMOTHER
LISA

Sometimes my life runs like a movie, in that I can be in the present but flashback instantly to the past.

That's what just happened to me, but in a good way.

In fact, in a way that was magical.

Because just last weekend, Francesca and I went to the wedding of my goddaughter Jessica, who is my best friend Franca's daughter.

And though Jessica just got married, I can jump back in time almost instantly, to well before Jessica was born.

To the first day I met her mother, my best friend.

It was in fact the first day of law school and Franca was reading a newspaper at her desk, and I happened to be walking behind her and I started reading over her shoulder. She looked up, and I realized I was being rude. I said, "I'm sorry, I was reading over

367

your shoulder."

She said with a smile, "I don't mind. My husband hates it, but I don't."

To which I replied, "My boyfriend hates it, but I don't."

And about a year later, we had both shed our respective husband and boyfriend, but our friendship remained.

We survived working at a law firm together, then subsequent marriages, and we both got pregnant about the same time, and I can jump back in time almost instantly to the day Jessica was born and I saw her in the hospital, only an hour old.

Franca and I used to say to each other, wouldn't it be funny if our kids played together?

It seemed only theoretical, like the hypos we talked about in law school.

But then, miraculously, it came true.

Our adorable babies ended up playing together, Francesca with her big blue eyes and blond curls, and Jessica with her big brown eyes and reddish brown curls.

And Franca asked me to be Jessica's godmother.

To the Italian people, that is a very sacred, close relationship.

Which is a line from *The Godfather.*

Truly I was honored to become Jessica's

godmother even though it included me vow-
ing in church that, should anything happen
to Franca, I would raise Jessica in the Catholic faith.

Which meant that I would have to become
a better Catholic.

I'm a fairly stinky Catholic, except when
the Pope was in town.

Then I became instantly religious, which
meant that I watched him on TV all day
and cried when that little boy sang.

But time took another jump forward, and
last weekend I found myself sitting next to
Francesca, herself all grown up, and we
both cried as we watched Jessica come down
the aisle on her wedding day, a natural
beauty in a simple but lovely wedding dress.

And Franca was so happy and so lovely,
in an elegant navy blue gown, and to me
she looked just as young as she did that first
day we met.

In fact, even younger because she has
come so much more into her own as she
has gotten older.

So have I, and I suspect so have you.

We're smarter than we used to be, aren't
we?

(Which is unfortunate because people
have stopped listening to us.

This would be the irony of life, especially

as a woman.

As soon as you know everything, you become the amazing disappearing middle-aged woman.

At least we can talk to each other.

Or write books like this.)

But back to the wedding.

I realized at that moment that Jessica was about the age that Franca and I were when we got married.

Whether it was the first or the second marriage doesn't really matter.

You start to forget which marriage it was, sometimes.

It's like your original hair color.

Who cares?

Anyway I realized how incredibly lucky and blessed the four of us women were. Me, to have been lifelong friends with Franca and to be godmother to her amazing daughter, and then to be sitting next to my own amazing daughter, all of us happy, healthy, and still together on this special day.

And I know it sounds crazy but it was a miracle to me, and it still is, reflecting on it now, because it was a dream of mine that really came true.

A dream that I would have a wonderful friend my whole life long.

A dream that I would have a wonderful

daughter whom I was so proud of.

A dream that I would have a wonderful goddaughter, who turned out so amazing in every way, and so much like her own mother, because they share the same generous heart.

We women are so lucky and so blessed that we remain friends for so long, and that we can share these special moments, not only with our own children, but with the children of our friends.

Whether they're godchildren or not doesn't matter, because truly it's a unique and singular experience to watch the children of the people you love grow into adults themselves.

And somehow time seems not to jump, or fly, but stand still, the past and the present conflating so that all time is the same, because that's the way we experience it.

And in my mind's eye, I can see Jessica walking down the aisle, and remember when I watched her in the sandbox at Sesame Place or fed her cooked pasta wheels in her car seat, right next to my own daughter, the two toddlers munching happily away, babbling to each other, and ultimately falling into an exhausted sleep after a trip to the zoo, Sesame Place, or even New York. Franca and I used to take them up there to

A beautiful day with Goddaughter Jessica, Bestie Franca, and Daughter Francesca

walk through FAO Schwarz because it had a big clock that played a song.

FAO Schwarz and the clock may be gone, but we all still remember the song.

And we remember those times, and they exist at the same time right now, in the present.

And when I saw Jessica coming down the aisle, I felt all the love, memories, and songs that the four of us have shared for the past thirty years, and it seemed to me something like a state of grace.

And I was so grateful for the simple, yet so profound, gift of being Jessica's godmother, and I realized that in the end, it was the goddaughter who gave the godmother a religious education, and not the other way around.

Wow.

I mean, oops.

That's not the way it's supposed to be.

But somehow I don't think the Pope would mind.

FRIENDSHIP ON THE FLIP SIDE
LISA

There are some things you learn only as you get older.

One is that the world will not end if you gain five pounds, or even ten.

The other is that girlfriends grow even more precious with time.

I wanted to take a serious moment, un-characteristic for me, to celebrate female friendship, especially after all of our estrogen has collectively evaporated.

I say this because I just got back from a Girls' Night Out with a group of friends, which was truly a Girls' Night In, because for some reason we never go to a restaurant. We always go to the same person's house because she is the best cook and loves to entertain, and even though we try to recip-rocate, she says no.

Or at least, that's our story and we're sticking to it.

The amazing thing about this group of

women friends is that we came together because of our children, and we stayed together, even though we have nothing in common and our children have long since flown the nest.

What brought us together?

Animals.

This group of six women, all of whom raised daughters who got bit by the horse bug and never let it go.

Daughter Francesca fell in love with horses at age ten, though she had never met a real horse, but only played with overpriced versions of them in plastic.

I'm talking, of course, about Breyer ponies, which are the equine equivalent of Barbies.

She had Barbies, too, but her interest in them waned, despite the fact that they had a fancy car and a dream house, which, by the way, were things that Francesca did not have growing up, as she was the only child of a broke single mother, who was struggling to become a published writer.

That would be me.

Francesca loved Breyer ponies, as well as My Little Ponies, then segued into reading books about horses and watching movies about horses, and in time it became pretty obvious that she was horse-crazy and I should really scrape some money together to get her riding lessons.

Because every mother knows that if you have any extra money, it is going for something the kids want, which is as God intended.

(Because somebody did it for you, didn't they?)

And so once a week, we drove an hour to take horseback-riding lessons in the country, and the more we did it, the more she loved it, by which point it began to be pretty clear to me that we should just move to the country, because it's cheaper, prettier, and as a writer, I could live in the middle of nowhere.

The stable provided Francesca with a horse to ride, but in time my writing career took off, thanks to all of you, and I was able to get her a real horse, and not only that, she got me interested in riding, so I started lessons, too. And about the same time, we looked around in the country for other people for her to ride with and we discovered something called Pony Club.

Pony Club is a nonprofit organization that was started in Britain but grew to attract horse-crazy kids, mostly girls, from everywhere and teach them the basics of horsekeeping.

Which is a lot more fun than housekeeping.

And they also get to form teams and compete against other Pony Clubs, just like a regular team sport, which means that Horse Moms do the things that Soccer, Baseball, Basketball, and Football Moms do, like drive kids to practice, make sure they have the right equipment, and desperately comb grocery-store shelves for healthy snacks in a world when unhealthy snacks are calling their name.

The only difference is that Horse Moms have to pick up manure.

Literally.

So Francesca joined Pony Club when she was about thirteen, and I met a circle of moms who had nothing in common but the fact that their kids were crazy about horses. We were a disparate group of Democrats, Republicans, Independents, nonprofit organizers, small-business owners, financial analysts, divorced and married, and we came from very different backgrounds. But like me, many of those moms had taken up riding themselves, if not out of curiosity, then in self-defense, because you'd better know what you're doing with a horse or you're liable to get kicked in the head.

And so began the origin of my friendship

with these women — Nan, Paula, Pam, Karen, and Jodi — and I'm surprised to report that this friendship has continued even though all of our daughters have grown up and all of our lives have changed in so many ways I can't begin to enumerate them, but they look a lot like the aisle of a greeting-card store; there are birthdays, anniversaries, second and third marriages, illness, deaths, and most lately, grandchildren.

God bless Hallmark.

I say this not in a denigrating way, because it came as a lovely surprise to me that if you stay close with a group of women, not only over ten years, but over twenty or even longer, you will share with them the major events in their lives, the ups and the downs, all of the tears and the joy, and the friendship will gain a momentum of its own, even if you don't see each other that often.

And so maybe three times a year, we all invade Karen's house and she makes us something delicious, and we've been doing this for so long that we hope she will make her hearty minestrone soup or her incredible corn salad.

When you crave dishes that your friends make, you're living your life right.

I just returned from one of those nights, and Karen made the hearty minestrone because it's that time of year, and we sat around the table and caught each other up on what our life is like, as well as what our kids' lives are like, and even what our horses' lives are like.

And our dogs and chickens, too.

Because animal people never know when to quit.

By the way, we still don't have anything in common, even after all these years, but that doesn't seem to matter. Nor does the fact that our kids are grown and that some of us don't even ride anymore.

We still have all of our differences, and in some ways we've become even more different. I didn't even realize how different until tonight, when the subject turned to politics, in an election season.

And even though we disagreed on fundamental issues, all of us love each other too much to let that part us.

We had each other.

And we had hearty minestrone.

And sometimes, that is more than enough.

YOU AREN'T WHAT YOU EAT
LISA

I'm here to tell you that life isn't fair.

John F. Kennedy said that first, but he wasn't talking about his weight.

I say this because I gained ten pounds in three months.

I don't know which number is worse, the ten or the three, but the fact that they occur together is the combination platter.

Or maybe I should stop with the food analogies.

Do you think it means anything that food is the first thing I think of?

Nah.

Or that I actually look forward to meals?

Yay, I get to eat!

Legit!

The ten pounds I gained were the same ten pounds it had taken me six months to lose, which I had accomplished by eating less and moving more. Not exactly an innovative approach, but the only one that's ever worked for me. I ate smaller portions, which took me time to get used to, and I increased my exercise level by biking twice a week instead of once. And making sure I used my treadmill desk in the On position.

Who knew.

I'm not completely surprised that I gained *some* weight because when the cold weather came on, I stopped biking, and when my deadline hit, I used the treadmill desk at a standstill, but still it seemed hard to explain.

I was only a little bad. I wasn't as bad as ten pounds' worth.

In other words, the punishment didn't fit the crime.

And by the way, before you flip over to that author photo and tell me that I don't need to lose weight, remember Photoshop.

I try to keep my author photo as fictional as my novels.

Also it's an ancient photo, which is intentional.

I'm frozen in time, somewhere around freshman year of high school.

(Please, I'm not the only author who does this. And the men are just as guilty as the women. You know who you are.)

But anyway, I just got back from my annual visit to the gynecologist, and she and I had our usual great talk, at least before she whips out the speculum.

When the speculum makes an appearance, we both shut up.

But before that, she always asks me how I'm feeling, then she works her way around to asking me if I've become sexually active since last year.

Uh, no.

The answer has been the same for six years now.

I always tell her that she was the last person who looked at my vagina.

In fact, my Pap smear counts as a date.

We both laugh.

But I'm not kidding.

Actually, I think it's been six years, but it could've been longer.

I forget the exact number.

It seems like a technicality.

In my last novel, I wrote a sex scene from memory.

It worked, for me.

But to stay on point, the gynecologist always tells me, as she did today, that if I become sexually active, intercourse may be painful.

I tell her that it's painful *not* having inter-course.

She laughs again.

Then I thank her for saying all the things she always says, and you have to be living under a rock or maybe never turning on a television to not know that intercourse at my age could be painful and that there are three hundred things they can prescribe for this condition, but none of them includes sleeping with Bradley Cooper.

Get with it, gynecology.

Anyway, so I started whining to her about the fact that I gained ten pounds, and she said that was to be expected because women over fifty burn one hundred fewer calories a day, no matter what they do.

Wait, what?

I didn't know that.

In other words, even if you eat the same amount and keep the same activity level, you won't lose the hundred calories a day that you used to.

That you deserve to lose.

That you sacrificed to lose.

And that, my friends, is UNFAIR.

I had read that your metabolism slows down as you get older, but I had never heard it quantified before.

I instantly thought of all the things that are a hundred calories, namely those little cookie snack packs that I'd finally cut out, which come premeasured for a hundred calories. Through sheer willpower, I'd stopped eating them, but it wasn't helping.

My metabolism was eating them for me.

I hate you, metabolism.

And then my gynecologist added the kicker, that after menopause, your body shape changes and your weight redistributes, so that the fat collects in your belly.

Nooooo!

That was news to me, too.

Because I'm getting a beer belly though I don't even drink beer.

I first noticed this on book tour, when I had to put on real clothes with actual waistbands, zippers, and buttons.

The frenemies of every middle-aged woman.

I had thought my newly chubby tummy was just part of my overall weight gain, but now I see that it's taken up permanent residence.

I hate you, menopause.

Well.

So I came home, texted all of my girlfriends on a group text, and whined to them about what I had learned from the gynecologist. And my girlfriends all texted me back, commiserating about metabolism, menopause, and speculums in general.

(Sorry. Specula.)

And we ended up kidding each other about our newly chubby bellies, and ultimately deciding by text that we would all save on heating bills until we dropped dead.

Then I set the phone aside, because it was time for lunch.

I started to make myself my usual salad, with honeycrisp apples, cheddar cheese, and walnuts.

And the more I chopped, the better I felt.

Truly, I wouldn't mind losing the ten pounds again.

But I'm not going to beat myself up about it, like I used to when I had a metabolism that actually did its job.

I may have my belly, but I also have the best girlfriends in the world, and we have shared so much over time.

They're my buffer against the unfairness of life.

They're what reminds me of what really matters.

Love.

I started this little book talking about changing the way I think about having sand in all the wrong places.

Remember, I flipped it.

It's really just the pixie dust of summer.

But I had forgotten my own lesson.

I needed to stop worrying about my belly.

And focus on my heart.
Amen.

ACKNOWLEDGMENTS

LISA AND FRANCESCA

This is where we get to say thank you, because thank-yous matter! We would like to express our love and gratitude to St. Martin's Press for supporting this book and its predecessors. First thanks to Coach Jen Enderlin, our terrific editor, as well as to the brilliant John Sargent, Sally Richardson, Jeff Dodes, Paul Hochman, Jeff Capshew, Stephanie Davis, Brian Heller, Brant Janeway, Lisa Senz, John Karle, Tracey Guest, Dori Weintraub, Michael Storrings, Anne-Marie Tallberg, Nancy Trypuc, Kerry Nordling, Elizabeth Wildman, Talia Sherer, Kim Ludlum, and the entire sales force. We got these books on the *New York Times* Best Sellers list, and we thank you for everything you do to support us!

We'd also like to thank Mary Beth Roche, Laura Wilson, Samantha Edelson, and St. Martin's audiobook division for giving us the opportunity to record our own audio-books. We love to do it, and we love audio-books!

Huge thanks and love to our amazing agents. Lisa would like to thank Robert Gottlieb of the Trident Media Group and his incredible team: Nicole Robson, Emily Ross, Alicia Granstein, Brianna Weber, Claire Roberts, and Sabine Jansen.

Francesca would like to thank Andrea Cirillo, Amy Tannenbaum, and Rebecca Scherer of Jane Rotrosen Agency. I'm thrilled to have found such a brain trust of wit and wisdom in these three incredible women — you have already exceeded my hopes for what a thoughtful, caring literary agent can be, and we're just getting started.

Thanks to *The Philadelphia Inquirer,* which publishes our "Chick Wit" column, and to our editor, the wonderful Sandy Clark.

One of the best people in the world is Laura Leonard, and her advice, friendship, and love sustain us. Laura, thank you so much for all of your great comments on and suggestions to this manuscript. We owe you, forever.

Love to our girlfriends, who let us tell stories about them! Lisa would like to thank Nan Daley, Paula Menghetti, Sandy Stein-gard, Rachel Kull, and Franca Palumbo. Francesca would like to thank Rebecca Harrington, Katy Andersen, Courtney Yip, Janie Stolar, Megan Amram, and right-hand man, Ryder Kessler — I endeavor to bring half the humor, insight, and wicked fun to these stories that you bring to my life. We're blessed in all of you.

Family is the heart of this book, because family is the heart of everything. Special thanks and love to Brother Frank, as well as the late Mother Mary and Big Frank Scottoline, though they are with us always.

Finally, thank you to our readers.

You're family, too.

ABOUT THE AUTHORS

Lisa Scottoline is a *New York Times* best-selling and Edgar award-winning author of more than twenty novels and coauthor of several humor memoirs in this series. She also writes a Sunday column for *The Philadelphia Inquirer*. She has 30 million copies of her books in print, and is published in thirty countries. She lives in the Philadelphia suburbs with an array of disobedient pets.

Francesca Serritella is a *New York Times* bestselling author and columnist for *The Philadelphia Inquirer*. She graduated cum laude from Harvard University, where she won the Thomas Temple Hoopes Prize, the Le Baron Russell Briggs Fiction Prize, and the Charles Edmund Horman Prize for her creative writing. She lives in New York with one dog and one cat, so far.